The Dynamics
of the Absurd
in the
Existentialist Novel

American University Studies

Series XIX
General Literature
Vol. 31

PETER LANG
New York • San Francisco • Bern • Baltimore
Frankfurt am Main • Berlin • Wien • Paris

Richard E. Baker

The Dynamics
of the Absurd
in the
Existentialist Novel

PETER LANG
New York • San Francisco • Bern • Baltimore
Frankfurt am Main • Berlin • Wien • Paris

Library of Congress Cataloging-in-Publication Data

Baker, Richard E.
  The dynamics of the absurd in the existentialist novel / Richard E.
Baker.
      p.   cm. — (American university studies. Series XIX, General
literature; vol. 31)
    Includes bibliographical references.
    1. Absurd (Philosophy) in literature.   2. Fiction—20th century—History
and criticism.   3. Existentialism.   I. Title.   II. Series.
    PN56.A24B34   1993   809.3'9384—dc20   92-38883
    ISBN 0-8204-2079-4   CIP
    ISSN 0743-6645

Die Deutsche Bibliothek-CIP-Einheitsaufnahme

Baker, Richard E.:
The dynamics of the absurd in the existentialist novel / Richard E. Baker. -
New York; Berlin; Bern; Frankfurt/M.; Paris; Wien: Lang, 1993
    (American university studies: Ser. 19, General literature ; Vol. 31)
    ISBN 0-8204-2079-4
NE: American university studies / 19

The paper in this book meets the guidelines for permanence and durability of
the Committee on Production Guidelines for Book Longevity of the
Council on Library Resources.

To Terri Baker

my beautiful and loving wife

ACKNOWLEDGEMENTS

I would like to thank the following people for their help through the years: Fred Boe, who encouraged my interest in comparative literature; José de Onís, who had faith in my abilities as a writer when others did not; and Hazel Barnes, who has been my friend and mentor for the last fifteen years. I would also like to give special thanks to all of the members on my dissertation committee: Warren Motte, Phyllis Kenevan, Mimi Mortimer, Arthur Boardman, John Stevenson, and Doug Burger.

The author wishes to thank the following publishers:

Excerpts from *Native Son* by Richard Wright. Copyright 1940 by Richard Wright. Copyright renewed 1968 by Ellen Wright. Reprinted by permission of HarperCollins Publishers.

Excerpts from *Native Son* by Richard Wright. Copyright 1940 by Richard Wright. Copyright renewed 1968 by Ellen Wright. Reprinted by permission of Jonathan Cape.

Excerpts from *The Last Gentleman* by Walker Percy. Copyright 1966 by Walker Percy. Reprinted by permission of Farrar, Straus & Giroux, Inc.

Excerpts from *The Last Gentleman* by Walker Percy. Copyright 1966 by Walker Percy. Reprinted by permission of Martin Secker and Warburg Limited.

CONTENTS

CHAPTER I

A SENSE OF THE ABSURD

Many existentialist writers in the twentieth century have defined the sense of the absurd: Miguel de Unamuno says it is the "tragic sense of life"[1]; Jean-Paul Sartre calls it "nausea"[2]; Richard Wright perceives it as the shame, dread, and fear that minorities experience in a dominant racist society, causing them to feel dispossessed and disinherited, thereby living in a "No Man's Land"[3]; and Walker Percy defines it as "alienation," "everydayness," and "homelessness."[4] In each instance it is the same dialectical experience of an individual trying to relate to an irrational world; and it is this way of existing, through a passionate choice, a revolt against any moral or metaphysical absolutes, and a total commitment to freedom, that becomes the focal point of existential thought. It is my intent in this book to explore the various characteristics of the absurd in order to better understand existentialist literature, especially the novel. In this way I hope to justify the matrix of the absurd, to project my thoughts and feelings into the reader's mind, until the reader has fully shared with me a world and an experience. All the novels contained in this book have these same attributes, and they all have one thing more: a flair for exhasuting the possible.

The most comprehensive essay written on the absurd is *The Myth of Sisyphus* by Albert Camus. It was Camus's intention specifically to describe and analyze the feelings, notions, and consequences of the absurd in order to provide modern readers with a practical, working definition of this ambiguous term, coinciding with the ambiguity of our being-in-the-world. Camus deliberately defines the absurd as "the divorce between man and his life, the actor and his setting."[5] Further on, he refines this definition:

> The absurd depends as much on man as on the world. For the
> moment it is all that links them together. It binds them one to
> the other as only hatred can weld two creatures together. This is
> all I can discern clearly in this measureless universe where my
> adventure takes place. (21)

It is because humans demand meaning in an unresponsive world that the
absurd exists, and concrete human problems arise in our acute awareness of
this dichotomy. The question of suicide arises for Camus, and whether the
absurd makes suicide justifiable. In response to this dilemma, Camus offers
two options: one can commit suicide and escape the situation, obliterating
the individual who feels and experiences the chaos in this world, or one can
thrust aside reason, take the leap, and funnel one's faith into divine channels,
hoping for eternal and divine intervention from what many call God;
however, Camus discards these two options, because they are not viable
solutions to the human plight, in favor of another possibility: keep the absurd
alive and in front of you, because this is the point at which life begins;
"unlike Eurydice, the absurd dies only when we turn away from it" (51-55).
This is the primary principle of the absurd. It must consciously be kept alive
within the individual and acknowledged, or there is a return to the tendencies
of suicide. In Camus's notion of things, the world is not absurd in itself, nor
is the absurd particular to the individual; but the absurd is the lack of communication between the two. Neither one can be discounted or reduced to
the separate reality of the other, but it is the interaction between the two
which gives rise to the absurd.

After these definitions, Camus enumerates six examples of how we encounter the absurd in ordinary life. First, he describes the experience of feeling the void and sincerely replying nothing when asked "what one is thinking" [...]. [T]hen it is as it were the first sign of absurdity" (12). Second, he
describes mechanical living, the deadening repetition of daily work, because
it fosters an onrush of futility; yet the "why" arises one day and consciousness awakens. Third, a person may become aware of time passing by
and thus living for the future. Again this is the divorce between an individual
and his or her worldly fate; people are caught in time and this makes no
sense. Fourth, the absurd may be experienced because nature is indifferent to
people, making the world seem strange, dense, or foreign even if familiar
objects are perceived. We are solitary in a world with which we have nothing in common. Likewise this is evident when there is an acute feeling of
isolation between ourselves and others; we are bewildered when we perceive

other human beings as nonhuman. And finally, there is the fact of death and the emotional response it evokes in us. It is inexplicable and makes no sense. We want to endure in life, but all people are nevertheless mortal.

Given the above, I want to see if Camus's criteria for the absurd show up in similar ways in other existentialist works as well. If Camus's notions and feelings of the absurd are viable, I can apply them to culturally diverse existentialist novels and obtain very important interpretive results; then, I want to see how Camus's ethics of either revolt, freedom, and passion lend possibilities to an existentialist solution as one confronts the absurd.

In the existentialist tradition, the novel occupies a key position. Simone de Beauvoir, in her article "Littérature et métaphysique," explains that

> while philosophy objectifies human reality, the novel captures it as it is lived, in all its subjective complexity and ambiguity. Only the novel [...] can evoke the original upsurge of existence. This is because it presents existence not as an object of thought but as action, feeling, and experience. It is thus a unique revelation of being, irreducible to a formula or to a system of philosophy.[6]

Although her definition was meant primarily to explain Sartre's novels, it is applicable to other existentialist novels as well. Since Beauvoir specifically describes the novel as a mode of presenting "human action, feeling, and experience," complete with "ambiguity," there are certain relationships to the sense of the absurd. Can positive results and aims (Beauvoir's "revelation of being") in other existentialist novels be derived from Camus's analysis and description of the absurd? Or is existentialism and its concept of the absurd as comfortless as some critics believe? This is where I want to push my investigation, to see what moral values the various protagonists in their confrontation with the absurd become lucidly aware of or attempt to deny. For the absurd by its very nature can produce either a suppression of its demand in people or a strong emotional impact upon its discovery. It follows that a sense of the absurd is a recognition that the world appears to be meaningless, yet one continues to live on as if it were not so, like the condemned prisoner who asserts the right to live even after sentence is passed. It is the confrontation of our desire for unity and clarity and the world's disunity and irrationality. The absurd for the existentialists is a revelation of certain facets of the human condition as revealed through the characters, places, events, and situations in their novels. It is a matter of analyzing the above criteria, making this a mode of discovery for any critique of the existentialist novel.

My first analysis of the absurd will concern Miguel de Unamuno, an early pioneer of existentialism. Is there a link between his work and that of

Camus's, since both write novels to illuminate their philosophy? Indeed, all of Unamuno's work centers around the quest for immortality, the battle between the head and the heart, and the absurdist features this dilemma presents.

In particular, *Mist*, the most problematic yet the most heralded of all his novels (Unamuno states that "no other work of mine has proved of more universal interest than *Mist*"[7]) subjectively presents the conflict between a person's head and heart. In fact, this novel is Unamuno's presentation of his lived subjectivity: the multiple contradictions between the rational mind and felt experience. Like Camus, Unamuno poses the problems of life and death in contradictory terms in order to show the dynamic tension inherent in our being-in-the-world.

Mist is also an inquiry into how an author can make fiction and reality blend together into a unique novel where the real and the imaginable become indistinguishable. Unamuno jokingly rejoices in fusing and confusing the tragic and the comic, making *Mist* into a tragic farce. In this way Unamuno hopes to create a legendary existence for himself as well as his characters. In fact, Unamuno proudly convinces himself that he has created his own genre apart from the novel—the "nivola"—a form where author and characters interact in order to create one another. The fictional beings become as real as the author who created them, and self-creation becomes a major theme in *Mist*. Of special interest to Unamuno is the ethical principle of revolt—a revolt against death—and his attempt to resolve this dilemma through the passionate creation of a work of art becomes tantamount to his quest for immortality.

As a corollary to the passion for creation, love becomes a major theme to break the tedium of living. Unamuno, like Camus, poses the absurdist problem of life as a routine, with the accompanying feelings and experiences of the anguish and boredom of mechanical living. And just as our passion for creativity helps us to break the tedium of life, likewise love goes hand in hand with our yearning for creativity and self-expression, espousing some of the problems that occur when one attempts to form an amorous relation with another person.

Can most of Camus's notions and consequences of the absurd be found concretely in *Mist*? Is the issue of suicide specifically addressed by Unamuno? If Unamuno seeks immortality and Camus wants quantitative living, do these two ideas overlap and redefine each other? And finally does the main protagonist of *Mist* fit into the Camusian experience and description of the absurd hero? These questions must be resolved in my analysis of *Mist*.

In my third chapter, I will discuss Jean-Paul Sartre's philosophical position in relation to the absurd, then develop this concept in terms of his novel *Nausea*. Some explanation of Sartre's ontology is necessary in order to form a basis from which to view his fiction and its absurdist features. Of course, *Nausea* illuminates the subjective experiences, feelings, and actions of Antoine Roquentin, the main character, that only Sartre's philosophy can objectify. Sartre's famous remark that "existence precedes essence" becomes concrete for the reader as Roquentin learns that things in the world, including himself, simply exist with no reason for being there. Also Sartre's philosophic terms being-in-itself (objects in the world) and being-for-itself (individual consciousness) are put into human terms as Roquentin embarks upon a journey into his true existential nature. This juxtaposition between objects in the world and a person becomes important in my discussion of the absurd. Once again it is essential to note the shared ideas of Sartre and Camus, as well as their differences. Sartre's discussion of our being gratuitous (*de trop*) is of the utmost importance, connecting Sartre and Camus, since the latter makes direct reference in *The Myth of Sisyphus* to Sartre's experience of "nausea."

My discussion of the absurd will center around three concentric layers of Roquentin's contingency of being-in-the-world. The first layer is the conflict between Roquentin's knowledge and reality; the second layer is the gap between his present and past (including that of an historical figure he is reading and writing about); and the third layer is the rift between facticity and transcendence. As each successive layer is stripped back, Roquentin's life is revealed to him.

Like Unamuno's novel *Mist*, self-realization through a work of art—music and literature—are important themes in *Nausea*, as is the theme of love. As Roquentin tries to rekindle his relationship with his former mistress in order to reconstruct his past, find possibilities from past adventures with her, and hopefully discover himself through being with her again, he embarks upon a new path in life as he sees their past and present relationship together in a new light.

Objects in the world, time, interpersonal relationships, Roquentin's body, his occasional feelings of wanting to vomit are all important aspects of *Nausea* and provide connections to *The Myth of Sisyphus*. Passion and creativity are the final themes which end *Nausea*, coinciding with what Camus sees as consequences of the absurd. The decisions Roquentin finally makes at the end of the novel will summarize all of the connections that I have made between *Nausea* and *The Myth of Sisyphus*. Here parallels can be seen between Sartre, Camus and Unamuno's work, yet there are specific differences as to what art accomplishes. Is art a refuge from the absurd? or is it part of the absurd experience which, when confronted, gives birth to creative thinking? These issues are specifically addressed in this chapter.

Chapter four contains an analysis of how *The Stranger* subjectively authenticates, painstakingly broadens, and concretely enriches the feelings of the absurd as contrasted to the philosophic notions of the absurd in *The Myth of Sisyphus*, leading up to the consequences exemplified in Camus's essay.

My discussion will first center around whether or not Camus can be considered an existentialist writer, when, in fact, he has denied being one. This entails a discussion as to what are the distinctive characteristics of Camus's writing which merit exclusion from or inclusion with other existentialist writers. Such distinguished critics as Hazel Barnes, John Cruickshank, and Philip Thody will be discussed, citing their reasons as to whether or not Camus can be considered an existentialist writer.

Of particular interest to my discussion is Camus's fame as a novelist, and Jean-Paul Sartre's critical comments upon the popularity of *The Stranger* in relation to *The Myth of Sisyphus*. From the basis of Camus's popularity as a novelist, he appears to be a moralist rather than a philosopher. An important introduction by Camus to the 1956 American University edition serves as the focal point for this argument. This theoretical position will lead me into the differences between thought and reality, between society's expectations and individuality, and the concomitant dilemma of choosing either a life of unity and conformity or one of authenticity.

My discussion elaborately develops Camus's six examples of experiencing the absurd in his essay, while making specific references to his novel. By this method, I can deduce some of Meursault's feelings and make parallels to the resulting consequences of the absurd. From Meursault's feelings as he experiences the void, mechanical living, the passage of time, nature and people making him feel inhuman, and finally death, these all become major themes in understanding the novel as it relates to the essay, since they were written as companion pieces.

Especially noteworthy, during Meursault's trial, is the remark he makes to the judge about the sun and why he killed the Arab; furthermore, the resulting laughter from the people in the courtroom is crucial to my discussion. Meursault's disquieting experience of the bright-hot Algerian sun plays an important symbolic role throughout the trial and the story as a whole, as does Meursault's former relationships with his mother, girl friend, friends, and social acquaintances. The farcical trial Meursault undergoes proves interesting as does the pronouncement of the death sentence. Meursault is condemned to death by guillotine, reflecting the problems of individuality versus society.

Meursault's final moments at the end of the novel are pertinent because Camus's feelings and ideas about death, religion, love, and friendship will harmonize and tie the novel together. This will become apparent by making a reference to Camus's discussion of the similarities between Christ and Meursault. Meursault's unwilling conference with the prison chaplain about God, the hereafter, and Marie will have prophetic ramifications as to Camus's moralist position in this novel.

My concluding remarks will center upon the similarities between Camus and Sören Kierkegaard. This will better explain Camus's moralist position in reference to Meursault and Christ, describing the various dynamic tensions which make up our radical freedom and enabling us to attain a more fulfilling life.

I will discuss Richard Wright's novel *Native Son* in chapter five. This novel is Wright's attempt to bring recognition of minority oppression into the modern world in America. Associating with the existentialist writers in France after World War II, Wright moved to Paris permanently because of the bigotry and the prejudice he experienced in the United States. Yet the ideas and feelings that Wright describes in this novel before meeting Jean-Paul Sartre, Albert Camus, and Simone de Beauvoir will coincide with many of their ideas: racial oppression is universal, and revolt, leading to freedom, is a necessary evil. This racial conflict is one aspect of the absurd, and I shall treat it as an important theme in this chapter.

The three chapters of Wright's novel—"Fear," "Flight," and "Fate"—will echo familiar terms that the existentialists use quite frequently in describing a person living in a world devoid of meaning and purpose. Bigger, like Meursault, is an outsider: a person caught between concepts called black and white. Wright's mental and physical description of Bigger living in a "No Man's Land" symbolizes Bigger's plight in life.

The humorous scene of the interaction between Bigger and his friend Gus, as they watch a skywriting plane at the beginning of the novel, will typify the absurd world of "ifs" that the Negroes live in on the South Side of Chicago, and, by implication, the United States. The fear and shame of being black fuels white racism. This important scene also foreshadows Bigger's revolt: he will exercise his radical freedom, commit a murder, and make passionate choices which will be balanced against his reflective thinking. Logical thinking is something he has been unable to accomplish throughout his life. This is mostly due to the contradictory nature of Bigger's idealized image of himself versus reality: white society presents ideals for him to aspire to, but they provide no means for him to attain these ideals, creating false hope for the Negroes. Does most of this novel coincide with Camus's notion of the absurd that people often negate one another? Since Bigger has received very little education and has to live in a squalid, cramped apartment with his family, who constantly bicker and try to emasculate him, is his life largely one of unreflective thinking because he is all emotion? Lacking a balance between his head and heart (using Unamuno's terminology) will Bigger's murder of Mary Dalton provide a balance between these two extremes and enable him to start living authentically?

This theme is further developed as Bigger fools the Dalton family and the police into believing that someone has kidnapped Mary. From this particular action will Bigger come alive for the first time in his life and freely create his life? This theme will be answered in terms of revolt, creation, and freedom in Bigger's quest for authentic existence.

Just as the heat of the sun becomes Meursault's undoing in *The Stranger*, so the heat from the fiery furnace in the Dalton's home will lead to Bigger's demise, relating to nature, another of Camus's examples of the absurd. In essence, does this theme of heat link the two novels together in reference to Camus's notion of death?

The denouement of the novel brings up sexual and racial issues: the farcical trial where Bigger is falsely accused, tried, convicted and sentenced to death for having first raped Mary, and then having to kill her in order to prevent her from telling anybody, represents the myth of the lust of black men for white women. Wright will use Bigger's lawyer to explain the plight of all Negroes in America, subject to reprisal from a white, dominant, racist society; yet the issue of rebellion to assert one's dignity is the focal point here.

As with Meursault, Bigger's final moment of self-realization will come about as he waits for his execution. Rejecting religion, his family, submissive Negroes, and racist whites, can Bigger create an identity for himself even if that identity is one of a murderer? Will he be able to cling to it and embrace it as his own? Bigger will also make an attempt to reach out to Max as a friend, but the lawyer will not understand Bigger's intentions. Instead Bigger's only true friend will be someone very unexpected.

Finally, I will relate Bigger's feelings, actions, and experiences throughout the novel to Wright's reasons for writing *Native Son*. Is there any connection between Wright and Camus in this context?

The final novel that I will discuss in chapter six is Walker Percy's *The Last Gentleman*. The theme of suicide plays a major role in this novel, providing a strong affinity to Camus's work.

Using Hazel Barnes's three characteristics of the literature of humanistic existentialism once again, I will examine whether this novel is indicative of this literature. Of central importance to my discussion is the overlap that exists between Percy's notion of "everydayness," "homelessness," and "alienation," and some of Camus's descriptions of the absurd in *The Myth of Sisyphus*. Altered terminology, but shared ideas, experiences, and feelings, become the focal point between the two authors. Subsequently, an analysis of Percy's earlier philosophical essays is necessary in order to understand certain facets of his fiction.

The Last Gentleman has mythical aspects, and certain fantastic objects—a telescope, a Trav-L-Aire camper, an Esso map, and a casebook—will help Will Barrett to chart his course in life. Once in the South, Will rediscovers his past, relating to Percy's philosophic idea of "repetition," which also must be elaborated upon because of its similarities to existentialist thought. Once home in Ithaca, Mississippi, at his old family home, Will confronts his past (Percy's idea of "repetition") and has a revelation similar to that of Sartre's

Roquentin. This becomes the turning point in the novel and whether Will becomes only a voyeur in life or an active participant. The thematic importance of authenticity and availability become the motors which drive this novel.

Three specific things—the ending of the novel, Jamie's death, and Sutter's desire to commit suicide—all have direct relevance to *The Myth of Sisyphus*. Both Camus and Percy make poignant assertions on ultimate values and what must be striven for incessantly. Percy especially has very specific words for those troubled people who are unwilling to face the unavoidable contradictions in life. This point will be discussed in terms of Will's contingency, responsibility, freedom, and dignity.

Finally, the dynamic tension between facticity and transcendence becomes paramount to my discussion, as does Percy's view of intersubjectivity. The bond that Will tries to form with Sutter leaves the novel open, but, as I will demonstrate, on a positive note. Again, an analysis of Percy's earlier essays afford possibilities of interpreting the ending of *The Last Gentleman*.

In my conclusion, I will tie together facets that these authors share in terms of *The Myth of Sisyphus* and the absurd, revealing the absurd as a matrix for experiencing, analyzing, and describing some of the ambiguities of life, yet providing viable existential alternatives. Since all the authors have used fiction to illuminate their philosophy, what does this tell us about these authors and their methodology? What can be said about these authors in terms of creation? Why do all of these authors describe people in search of love, self-realization, self-creation, or friendship? By using the final narrative at the end of Camus's essay, I hope to answer these questions, concluding my discussion of the absurd on a positive note.

10

NOTES

Miguel de Unamuno, *The Tragic Sense of Life,* trans. Anthony Kerrigan (Princeton: Princeton UP, 1972) 39.

2 Jean-Paul Sartre, *Nausea,* trans. Lloyd Alexander (New York: New Directions Publishing Corp., 1964) 129.

3 Richard Wright, introduction, "How 'Bigger' Was Born," *Native Son* (New York and Evanston: Harper & Row, 1940) vii-xxxiv.

4 Walker Percy, *The Message in the Bottle* (New York: Farrar, Straus, and Giroux, 1975) 24; 83-89.

5 Albert Camus, *The Myth of Sisyphus and Other Essays,* trans. Justin O'Brien (New York: Alfred A. Knopf, 1975) 6. In further references to this work in CHAPTER I, I will use page numbers only.

6 Quoted in Robert Ellis, *The Tragic Pursuit of Being: Unamuno and Sartre* (Tuscaloosa and London: Alabama UP, 1988) 53.

7 Miguel de Unamuno, *Mist, Novela/Novela*, trans. Anthony Kerrigan (Princeton: Princeton UP, 1976) 22.

CHAPTER II

MIST

On the basis of his position in *The Tragic Sense of Life* (1913), Miguel de Unamuno has been identified as an existentialist writer by such critics as Alfred Stern[1] and Robert Olson.[2] It is in the second chapter of that work that he rejects Descartes's *cogito* in favor of *sum, ergo cogito*; and with this new formulation he was a pioneer of the basic existential principle that human existence precedes essence,[3] bringing existentialism into the twentieth century from the nineteenth century and developing Sören Kirkegaard's notion of philosophy. From this principle, Unamuno wants to show that the goal of individual consciousness is to be unique and singular, and from this goal there exists a perpetual desire to feel and to perceive. It is Unamuno's intention to stress human existence as nothing less than the total person—passions, will, intuition, fears, hopes, and desires—rather than the reduction to an abstract subject, which indicates that Unamuno anticipated the existentialist movement.

Briefly stated, Unamuno's existential ontology in this book centers around two irreducible points: the consciousness of one's personal existence and one's terror of nothingness. According to Unamuno, a person's most profound desire is for eternal life, and this is the essence of life or of any knowledge which an individual might possess about himself or herself:

> For the present let us agree on this intense suspicion that the
> longing not to die, the hunger for personal immortality, the
> striving to persevere indefinitely in our own being, all of which

is, according to the tragic Jew, our very essence, constitutes the affective basis of all knowledge and the personal inner point of departure for any and all human philosophy wrought by man for his fellows. (*Tragic* 42)

Throughout most of his life, Unamuno was perpetually concerned with the question of immortality. Because of his Catholic upbringing in Spain, he was initially secure in his belief in the immortality of the soul; but when he began college as a teenager in Madrid, his faith dwindled. As he read Kant and Hegel, he began to experience a conflict between his faith and his reason, with reason soon taking priority over his faith.[4] The final outcome can be seen in this passage:

The Catholic solution to our problem, to our unique vital problem, the problem of the immortality and eternal salvation of our soul, satisfies the will, and, therefore, satisfies life; but, in attempting to give a basis in reason by means of dogmatic theology it fails to satisfy reason. And reason has its own exigencies, as imperious as those of life. (*Tragic* 86-87)

Since Unamuno liked to refer to himself as a "man of flesh and blood," he used concrete terms to express himself. Consequently he described the confrontation between reason and faith as a clash between the head and the heart. Unamuno was a Catholic with his heart, but not with his head, and he was not able to sacrifice his rational side.[5] For this reason the Catholic church proclaimed him a heretic and discouraged anybody from reading his works, especially *The Tragic Sense of Life*.[6]

Wanting to live eternally in both body and spirit, the contradiction between life and death became paramount for Unamuno:

Some readers may see a basic contradiction in everything I am saying, as I long on the one hand for unending life, and on the other claim that this life is devoid of the value assigned to it. A contradiction. I should say so! The contradiction between my heart which says *Yes*, and my head which says *No*! (*Tragic* 17)

As a result, the contradiction between his head and his heart became an insoluble one for him: "And now we have reached the very depths of the abyss: the irreconcilable conflict between reason and vital feeling" (*Tragic* 138). This conflict is what Unamuno terms the "tragic sense of life":

> For to live is one thing and to know is another, and, as we shall see, there may be such an opposition between the two that we may say that everything vital is, not only irrational, but anti-rational, and everything rational is anti-vital. And herein lies the basis for the tragic sense of life. (*Tragic* 39)

Unamuno's ontology, from start to finish, is a study of nothingness in relationship to human existence. "As one delves within oneself, the deeper one goes the more one discovers one's inanity, the truth that one is not altogether oneself, not what one wants to be, and, in short, that one is nothing" (*Tragic* 151-52). Yet it is these antithetical properties of nothingness and human existence which creates the hunger for immortality, or the being which it is not—an absence of being. Thus we see that for Unamuno human existence cannot be explained without contradictions. In the introduction to the 1972 English translation of *The Tragic Sense of Life*, Salvador de Madariaga stresses this point, "He was aware of his contradictions, indeed he gloried in them for they were tokens of his existence as a human being [...]."[7] Unamuno explains this position:

> I shall be told that mine is an untenable position, that a foundation is needed upon which to build our actions and our works, that it is impossible to live by contradictions, that unity and clarity are essential conditions for life and thought, and that it is imperative to unify the latter. And so we are back where we started from. For it is precisely this inner contradiction which unifies my life and gives it a practical purpose. (*Tragic* 282-83)

However, this contradictory position is not a bleak view of life because we can see that the tragic sense of life does intensify consciousness:

> There is something which, for want of a better name, we shall call the tragic sense of life, and it carries along with it an entire conception of the Universe and of life itself, an entire philosophy more or less formulated, more or less conscious. (*Tragic* 21)

"For want of a better name," this is significant. Unamuno describes his philosophy as "the tragic sense of life," but the contradiction between the head and the heart can also be termed the absurd because the absurd is the contradiction between a person's intent and reality; and this contradiction also produces an acute conscious awareness of existence. Here we can see the initial parallel to Camus and *The Myth of Sisyphus* when Unamuno states: "Since we live solely from and by contradictions, since life is a tragedy and the tragedy is in the perpetual struggle without hope of victory, then it is all a contradiction" (*Tragic* 17). Camus says something strikingly similar: "That evidence is the absurd. It is that divorce between the mind that desires and the world that disappoints, my nostalgia for unity, and this fragmented universe and the contradiction that binds them together."[8]

For Camus and Unamuno, in their quest for authentic existence, time and death become threatening to all human values. Unamuno craves immortality and does not want to return to nothingness; passion and revolt become his imperative for moral action: to act in such a manner that final annihilation is an injustice, "and above all, we must feel and act as if an endless continuation of our earthly life were reserved for us after death; and if nothingness is our fate instead, let us not make it a just fate" (*Tragic* 281). On the other hand, Camus could not envision immortality, accepting the finality of death "in which everlasting nothingness seems the only reality" (*Myth* 25); yet he also believes that "what counts is not the best living but the most living" (61). (In many respects Camus's desire for quantitative living is a yearning for immortality.) Moreover Camus proclaims estimable the struggle for life to be the supreme victory, using the consequences of passion, revolt, and freedom. I can summarize these two attitudes of life in terms of the absurd: Unamuno believes the absurd to be our hunger for immortality against the evidence of attaining it, "and this absurdity can rest only on the most absolute uncertainty" (*Tragic* 115-16), which becomes the clash between our head (logic and reason) and heart (vital feeling, passions, will, and intuition); Camus believes the absurd to be "the confrontation of this irrational and the wild longing for clarity whose call echoes in the human heart" (*Myth* 21). This last statement by Camus is significant because he does imply that there is a contradiction between the head and the heart which also creates the absurd. Hence the two men's differences seem to be a matter of terminology, for they share much in common: both men scorned death, revolted against it, and passionately affirmed life. Camus summarizes this attitude at the end of *The Myth of Sisyphus*:

> Sisyphus woke up in the underworld. And there, annoyed by an obedience so contrary to human love, he obtained from Pluto permission to return to earth in order to chastise his wife. But when he had seen again the face of this world, enjoyed water

and sun, warm stones and the sea, he no longer wanted to go
back to the infernal darkness. (120)

Given the above, Unamuno's work can be profitably examined from the
point of view of Camus's sense of the absurd, especially the novels. Camus
states that "the novel has its logic, its reasonings, its intuition, and its postu-
lates" (*Myth* 100). A good novel, according to Camus, must lucidly present
both the logical and the intuitive.

Unamuno makes the novel one of his primary sources of artistic expression in order to reveal his intuition of a person's lived subjectivity in a human setting, not an impersonal abstraction whereby ideas replace people. In
other words he emphasizes the concept of objectivity to be the greatest fal-
lacy in art. All art, he says, is the personal expression of the author, and is,
therefore, autobiographical.[9] Camus evokes a similar notion: "The idea of
art detached from its creator is not only outmoded; it is false" (*Myth* 96). The
novel, in Unamuno's sense of the word, keeps in touch with human experience, yet Unamuno describes his novel as a "nivola" (as opposed to
"novela"). The theme of his "nivola" is human consciousness, which he describes as a sort of nothingness that must be given some sort of being; and
this being will be a profound self-consciousness. In *How to Make a Novel*
(1926), Unamuno explains that everything in life is fiction and for a novel to
succeed it must be like life; this is how artistic endeavors are made manifest.
Leon Livingstone, a critic of Unamuno's work, explains:

> If all life is fiction, and fiction therefore life, the highest form of
> fiction is that which is deliberate, freed from the contingency of
> existence in the "real" world. It is more than reality itself, for
> reality is always less than it could or would be. Herein enters
> the role of art.[10]

Consequently, by denying the objective dimensions in life, Unamuno can
be the creator of the legendary existence of others. The "nivola," in his concept of the word, is essentially guided by freedom of invention. By having
the fictional world envelop the real world, Unamuno hopes to be taken into
the subjectivity of his readers, whereby he can achieve being in others, and
hence a sense of worth—his craving for immortality. Art is born in the quest
for authentic existence and, in this way, Unamuno achieves his hunger for
immortality by fictionalizing this intense desire in his novels.

This helps us to understand an essential characteristic of humans: imagination, since we are in fact imaginative people—some more and some less.

Julian Marias, another prominent critic of Unamuno's work, summarizes this attitude concerning Unamuno's fictional characters in relationship to real human beings: "The character in being fictitious—as opposed to the stone, which has a physical being, or desire, which belongs in the category of psychic being—and what his author imagines in him is precisely the full and true reality which is man and man's life."[11] The author, therefore, creates characters who in turn create the author, "'*To be or not to be!*' said Hamlet, one of the protagonists who invented Shakespeare."[12]

In writing about thought and existence, Unamuno creates an essence for himself (a novelist), and by making himself a novelist, he makes himself one with the reader. "And only by the novelist and the reader of the novel making themselves one do they save themselves from their radical solitude. In the degree that they make themselves one they become actual and present and thereby eternal" (Unamuno, *How* 479). Therefore, the novel can be similar to one's own experiences in human life from which it in fact derives, and it can aid us in understanding the essence of the way of being which make up an individual. Marias again points this out explicitly in reference to Unamuno's novels:

> The purpose of the existential or personal novel is to make plain
> to us a person's history, letting his intimate movements develop
> before our eyes, in broad daylight, and thus uncovering his ul-
> timate nucleus. The purpose is, simply, to show human exis-
> tence in all its truth. (*Miguel* 61)

To what extent does one find evidence of the absurd (as previously explained) in Unamuno's novels? An examination of *Mist* will provide some answers.

As *Mist* begins, Victor Goti, a fictional character, comes to life in order to undermine Unamuno's duties as a prologist. In this first person authoritative prologue, Victor insists that he and Unamuno are somehow related and both are privy to certain information: Victor's role, like Unamuno's, is dual because he is a man with his own story to tell and he is writing a novel. All of this becomes a distinct effort on Victor's part to convince us of the reality of a fictional being, who is just as real as his creator. Victor goes out of his way to insist that this "nivola" is a "tragic farce"; he explains this by saying it is "confounding" and a series of opposites: there can be no humor without "indiscretion," and laughter provokes "vomiting" rather than acting as an "aid to digestion." Victor goes on to say that Unamuno is going to fuse and confuse the comic with the tragic and reality with fiction. Victor ends by insisting that he, personally, will clarify the ambiguous matter of Augusto Perez (the protagonist) and the events surrounding Augusto's attempt to commit suicide.

The next part of *Mist* is a post-prologue written by Unamuno himself, in which he says that he is now in a difficult position in regards to Victor's conclusions about Augusto's death. In fact, Unamuno admonishes Victor, then, laughs and says if Victor doesn't "tread softly" in questioning his (Unamuno's) authority as author, Unamuno will do away with Victor as he did with Augusto. All of this is meant to leave Unamuno's readers with varying degrees of doubt regarding his power to control his fictional characters.

After the prologues, the tale unfolds concerning Augusto and his constant worry about whether he exists or not. Stepping out of his door one day and deciding to take a walk, Augusto is undecided as to which direction he will go. Ultimately he resolves that he will follow the first dog that comes along; however, encountering first a beautiful young woman, Eugenia, he follows her around town, then follows her home and falls in love with her without actually meeting her formally. Augusto describes his existence prior to the discovery of Eugenia as a life of boredom, and it becomes obvious that Augusto (his name literally reveals his "august" attitude) comes alive or realizes his existence, to a certain extent, because of his infatuation with Eugenia (her name literally means happy or good birth); yet he wonders how he can love someone he doesn't know, so he convinces himself that knowledge will come later (the existentialist account of life as a temporal process, where we make our essence—who we are—by the ongoing choices we make) because mist and vagueness are better for now when one is in love:

> *My own humble, humdrum, routine life constitutes a Pindaric ode made up of the day's endless detail. Daily detail! Give us today our daily bread! Give me, Lord, the endless detail of every day! The only reason we don't go under in the face of devastating sorrow or annihilating joy is because our sorrow and our joy are smothered in the thick fog of endless daily detail. All life is that: fog, mist. Life is a nebula. (34)*

Here we see the existentialist claim that one can never be anything because one's life is always a constant "becoming" —a temporal process—or absurd in its lack of fixed human nature or essence.

These actions and musings by Augusto, provide a link with Camus's description of the absurd, mechanical living, where one day the "why" arises and "inaugurates the impulse of consciousness." Augusto is so conditioned by his quotidian routine (the mist of existence obscuring the meaning of daily life) that his first intent is to follow a dog around town for some sense of direction and purpose, yet reality, in the person of beautiful Eugenia, steps in by chance and reflections on the absurdity of life spring forth. He falls in love, and the mist of his boring existence clears away: *"And what is love? Is it not perhaps the juice squeezed from tedium"* (48)? Augusto now has a limited but passionate awareness of his existence, trying to direct his life in more constructive ways (rather than following dogs around town), because he attempts to make a liaison with Eugenia. Sartre's comments are appropriate here: "Man makes himself. He isn't ready made at the start. In choosing his ethics, he makes himself, and force of circumstances is such that he can not abstain from choosing one. We define man only in relationship to involvement."[13]

Later in the fourth chapter as Augusto muses to himself again, we get a glimpse of other things besides love that can spring from a conscious awareness of tedium—the creation of novels: *"Most of us, nearly all of us, are unconsciously bored. Tedium is the substratum of life, and it is from tedium that most games have been invented, games and novels—and love"* (47).

In the jumbling of opposites between fiction and reality, Unamuno seems to step into the novel, through the fictional character of Augusto, to proclaim how he (Unamuno) has also confronted the absurd in terms of mechanical living. In this sense Unamuno's consciousness of the absurd finds itself passionately entrenched in recreating the reality which is expressly his own: the love of creating a novel because of his hunger for immortality. We find parallels here to Camus's view of the absurd because he also says, "In this regard the absurd joy par excellence is creation" (*Myth* 93). And a few pages later Camus also adds that "creation follows indifference and discovery. It marks the point from which absurd passions spring and where the reasoning stops." Just as Augusto has discovered himself through his love for Eugenia by letting his passion come forth to stop his reason, Unamuno does the same: he discovers himself as he creates his novel.[14] Camus says, "The novel in question is the instrument of that simultaneously relative and inexhaustible knowledge, so like that of love. Of love, fictional creation has the initial wonder and fecund rumination" (*Myth* 101). In other words, this passion is a consequence of the absurd which stops the mechanicalness of both the author and character's personalities, caught in repetitive living, and allows them to authentically claim their being-in-the-world. In point of fact, Augusto and Unamuno attempt to create meaning in the face of the absurd, drawing from it a passion for living. This passion—love for a woman and love for creating a novel—is what determines the actions both men will take as this "nivola" unfolds.

As the plot develops, Augusto finally gets to meet Eugenia one day while pining around in front of her house because a bird cage accidentally falls on him. Taking the bird cage to her door, he meets Eugenia's Aunt Ermelinda and Uncle Fermin, who are taken with Augusto (he is young and wealthy); and they consent to arrange a meeting between their niece and him. The meeting of the young couple can be defined in existentialist terms: since Eugenia is constantly gazing at Augusto, the existentialist concept of the "look" (an individual perceiving the "Other" as an object) becomes evident. Eugenia sees Augusto only as an object, but Augusto determines that this look must be love; for he thinks that it is through love that he will overcome his existential nothingness, that he will find a being in Eugenia's love for him. Augusto thinks that love gives him bulk and substance.

Feeling the urge to confide in someone about this new-found love, Augusto seeks out Victor to converse with him. In their many conversations we get a glimpse of the plot of *Mist*. Victor confesses that in order to forget about his own existential anguish, he has started to write a novel. He informs Augusto that he calls his novel a "nivola," and since Victor has invented a new genre, he has the right to make up the rules of the "nivola" as he sees fit. Here again we see an author attempting to project himself novelistically ("nivolistically"), so the character discovers himself by creating of his own life a novel-within-a-novel. The noteworthy part of Victor's "nivola" will be that the plot will unravel itself while he writes it, implying that a novel should imitate life itself, or "the novel, like life, must create itself as it proceeds" (Livingstone 98). This fictional existence by author and character becomes the basic plot of *Mist* because Victor and Unamuno are essentially writing the same novel. It is at this point that Augusto achieves some reflective knowledge of his own world as in a "nivola," and he wonders if he is anything more than the dream of "somebody else" (the "Other" in existentialist terms) in some "nivola."

As Augusto's knowledge of Eugenia's life surfaces (she has another suitor), his passion begins to wane, and there is a swing from his heart to his head, fulfilling his prophecy that knowledge will come later. Augusto now invents a new phrase *Amo, ergo sum* ("I love, therefore I am") to define his existence. A little later in the novel, this rationalization of love is taken to such an extreme that Augusto falls in love with every female he sees. Like Don Juan, Augusto multiplies what he cannot unify. Augusto falls in love with his old servant, Liduvina; the laundry girl, Rosario; and some of the pretty young women walking on the streets in town. In these examples we now see that Augusto's passion for love is inauthentic because it is a convenient and easy rationalization. The tedium of living is displaced by love, but it now becomes a mental or theoretical love which, as stated before, makes his existence only partial. Victor makes this explicit when he tells Augusto:

> Especially in your case, since your kind of falling in love is purely cerebral, or as we say, in the head. [...]
> And if you push me to it, if you drive me to tell the whole truth, I'll point out that you yourself are no more than a figment of imagination, a pure idea, a fictional being.... (82)

Augusto cannot make up his mind exactly who he really loves, which has the effect of devaluing his passion. He doesn't want anyone to define his words or actions so he can remain in a state of pretense. By imaginatively loving every woman, he loves nobody (like T. S. Eliot's Prufrock); therefore, Augusto cannot balance the two extremes (his head and heart) in order to become an authentically whole person. His type of love (the head) is insufficient since it is a love without reciprocity from the other person. In existentialist terms he is operating in bad faith, oscillating between facticity and transcendence (going from the desire to feel his body through the passion of love to pure intellect) and hiding behind a role that he has invented. Sartre clarifies this type of situation in his philosophical work, discussing a woman on a date with a man for the first time:

> But then suppose he takes her hand. This act of her companion risks changing the situation by calling for an immediate decision. To leave the hand there is to consent in herself to flirt, to engage herself. To withdraw it is to break the troubled and unstable harmony which gives the hour its charm. The aim is to postpone the moment of decision as long as possible. We know what happens next; the young woman leaves her hand there, but she *does not notice* that she is leaving it. She does not notice because it happens by chance that she is at this moment all intellect. She draws her companion up to the most lofty regions of sentimental speculation; she speaks of Life, of her life, she shows herself in her essential aspect—a personality, a consciousness. (*Essays* 161)

Something very similar to this happens when Augusto is with Rosario; they are attracted to each other, but Augusto tries to pretend he is all intellect. He caresses and kisses her then mysteriously commands her to leave, concealing from himself his own bad faith and justifying his physical attraction for her intellectually. Afterwards he thinks to himself:

> We men do nothing but lie and give ourselves airs. Words were invented for exaggerating our feelings and impressions—probably so we'd believe in them...words and speech and all the other conventional means of expressing ourselves, such as kissing, embracing.... Every one of us does nothing but act out his role in life. We're all so many characters in a drama, mere masks, actors! (135-36)

As Camus says, the absurd fades from sight when one fails to confront it. In this manner Augusto accepts a devalued, pretentious love to define his existence and thereby evades a significant part of human reality. His intent to love no longer clashes with reality since he assumes, in bad faith, that any woman he chooses must love him too; facticity gives way to transcendence and this attitude initiates actions which cause him to confront once again his nothingness. This becomes apparent when Augusto tries to help Eugenia financially by redeeming and making as a present to her the mortgage on her house. She logically assumes that he is trying to buy her love:

> "Ah, now I see your game! You are to play the part of the victim, you are to be the martyr! You reserve for yourself the role of hero! Keep the house, I tell you. It's a present from me."
> "Eugenia, Eugenia!"
> "That will do!"
> And without another word or look that pair of fiery eyes vanished.
> Augusto was stunned. He could not be sure that he existed. (98)

Inevitably, all of Augusto's advances towards Eugenia are spurned because she loves another, Mauricio, and she intends to marry him instead. It is at this point that Augusto confronts the absurd again—his love failed to give him a being—yet he swings back to the emotional side of life (the heart), with the result that he contemplates suicide. Augusto's state of mind suggests *The Myth of Sisyphus*, where Camus states:

> There is but one truly serious philosophical problem and that is

suicide. Judging whether life is or is not worth living amounts to answering the fundamental question of philosophy. [...] These are the facts the heart can feel; yet they call for careful study before they become clear to the intellect. (*Myth* 3)

A little further Camus also says:

Does the absurd dictate death? This problem must be given priority over others, outside all methods of thought and all exercises of the disinterested mind. [...] It is always easy to be logical. It is almost impossible to be logical to the bitter end. Men who die by their own hand consequently follow to its conclusion their emotional inclination. (*Myth* 9)

From Camus's concept of the absurd and suicide, there is a direct link to *Mist*, involving Augusto's passion taken to the extreme; and it can be compared to the conversation that Victor and Augusto are having (Chapter 30) in reference to other people's laughter and ridicule, making Augusto think of suicide. Briefly stated, Augusto is shattered by his loss of Eugenia, and Victor comes to visit him. To comfort him, Victor makes jokes by telling Augusto there will be other women, yet Augusto is feeling existential anguish because others have laughed, scorned, and mocked him; he feels it's as if they wanted to prove he doesn't exist, and he would like to think that he is not the ridiculous object that others perceive him to be. Thus, Augusto is torn in two: he relies on others for his existence, but they threaten to destroy him through their ridicule and laughter; to console himself he talks about suicide with Victor.

To change Augusto's mind, Victor tells him this is precisely the time for jokes by explaining that although laughter can be "caustic" and "corrosive," it can also be redeeming through acceptance. For while the laughter of others can be derisive and threatening, especially if it is meant to dehumanize, from a subjective standpoint the laughter can help one to experience one's existence through an acceptance of one's contingency. The perception of this derisive laughter is proof of existence as an individual; it must not be denied.

We can see this in other terms as well when Victor tells Augusto "to devour" others or "be devoured" by them, yet he also adds a third possibility: "devour yourself." By this statement Victor means "to make a fool of yourself" because this devouring of yourself reveals a profound self-consciousness (210). A clue to understanding this reasoning can be seen in *The Tragic Sense of Life* when Unamuno speaks of Don Quijote. Unamuno explains that

Don Quijote will triumph over himself by laughing at himself and making himself laughable. In this way inns will be castles because the world will be as Don Quijote wants it to be. Don Quijote, through the act of self-creation, works toward a project of existence in which he defines himself by the heroic deeds he will attempt to accomplish, whether they seem foolish to others or not. By making himself look ridiculous, he will triumph, proving that public approval is an inferior value. In Kierkegaard's terms, "truth is subjectivity."[15]

Victor goes on to explain that laughter and jokes are meant to confuse, "To confuse sleep with being awake, fiction with reality, the true with the false" (210). If Augusto is to have an authentic existence, he must not refuse to accept this part of life, but accept these confusing opposites and contradictions in order to form the basis of his personality.[16] He must look at his life subjectively, not as others see him. And here is the key to Unamuno's view of the absurd: the confusion of reality with fiction and seriousness with humor takes us back to a tension of opposites in the prologues (Victor and Unamuno's humorous dispute over Augusto's death), which also takes us back to the beginning of Augusto's story. Augusto had fallen in love with his own fantasy of Eugenia, and all of Augusto's problems stemmed from his inability to discern reality from fantasy or the dictates of the head from those of the heart. This is the absurd principle that Unamuno provides in this "nivola." This is the mist of the absurd: the contradictory nature of life through the clash of opposites (the head and the heart).

In Augusto's attempt to make one momentous decision concerning his life, since he is now armed with the knowledge of how the head and heart clash, he goes to Unamuno to tell him he will commit suicide (Chapter 31). In this scene, Unamuno intervenes as a character in his own fiction, and Augusto is made to intervene in Unamuno's life outside of the novel. Smiling enigmatically, Unamuno tells Augusto repeatedly that he cannot commit suicide, for Augusto is merely a fictional character in a "nivola"; Augusto is now privy to the secret Victor and Unamuno shared. In this constant pull between opposites—between fiction and reality, the head and the heart—Augusto mocks Unamuno and tells him that perhaps the author is merely a pretext for bringing Augusto's story into the world:

> "Could it not possibly be, my dear Don Miguel," he added, "that it is you and not I who are a creature out of fiction, the person who actually does not exist, who is neither living nor dead? Could it not possibly be that you are a mere pretext for bringing my story to the world..." [?] (219)

In response to Augusto's speech, Unamuno becomes extremely upset, agitated and nervous. He tells Augusto that as a fictional character he cannot commit suicide, because Unamuno will kill him instead. This awakens in Augusto his desire for life and he pleads for Unamuno to spare him, but to no avail. In one last threatening speech for life Augusto tells Unamuno:

> "So you won't let me be myself?" he said to me. "So you won't let me be myself, emerge from the mist, live, live, live at last, see myself, touch, listen, feel, hurt, be myself! So you won't have it? You want me to die a fictional being! I am to die as a creature of fiction? Very well, my lord creator, Don Miguel de Unamuno, you will die too! You, too! And you'll return to the nothingness from which you came! God will cease to dream you! You will die, yes, you will die, even though you don't want to. You will die, and so will all those who read my story, every one, every single one, without a single exception!" (226)

The irony is that Unamuno now becomes another ridiculous character acting out the role of an author, in spite of his attempt to show the unfairness of death by confirming his own being-in-the-world as his character Augusto had attempted. This is one of the most paradoxical scenes in Unamuno's novels because it oscillates between the head and the heart, between an author and his fictional character, thereby fusing and confusing fiction and reality into a novel of unique proportions. Not only are we all subject to others' interpretation of ourselves, but if we submit to the role they assign us, we are living in bad faith. Those who don't submit and do battle, like Don Quijote, are those who refuse to be merely an object in the world for others. This leads us to revolt—another reaction to the absurd that Camus addresses.

In *The Myth of Sisyphus* Camus describes the absurd as a response to our awareness of death and the feeling it evokes in us. In truth there is no real human experience of death because experience refers to that which is lived and made conscious; therefore, we can have no consciousness of our own death, nor of others. We cannot transpose our realization of their death into the understanding of our own nonexistence. In *Mist*, Augusto is suddenly confronted with the absurd feeling of death when Unamuno tells Augusto that he will not commit suicide, but will die by the author's own choosing. Unamuno is using the novel here in order to probe into that unique experience of death which can never be fully understood. Augusto, in making survival paramount, revolts against his author and seeks to perpetuate himself in the flesh. For Augusto, this revolt, taking the form of defiance, gives life its value. Since Augusto must die, he says that every reader of this novel will die because we are all "nivolistic" creatures. Hence we, as readers, all share the dilemma of Augusto, for we must reject death while still being aware of it. Augusto finally tells Unamuno:

> "[H]e who creates himself, dies. You'll die, Don Miguel, you will die, and so will all those who imagine me, they too will die." [...]
> This supreme effort in his passionate striving for life—or yearning for immortality—left poor Augusto totally exhausted. (227)

The above passage is echoed by Camus when he states:

> The absurd man can only drain everything to the bitter end, and deplete himself. The absurd is his extreme tension, which he maintains constantly by solitary effort, for he knows that in that consciousness and in that day-to-day revolt he gives proof of his only truth, which is defiance. (*Myth* 55)

Finally, Augusto goes home, like a condemned prisoner returning back to his cell after judgment is passed, convinced that he will not be able to commit suicide. Another critic of Unamuno's work, Alexander Parker, explains Augusto's suicide attempt in terms of the head in revolt against the heart:

> The death wish of Augusto is the desire for peace through the surrender of the conscious reason; but the Unamuno *agónico* cannot allow his creation to give up the struggle so readily. He therefore turns Augusto's death into the *agonía* of one decreed from above, against the injustice of which the victim rebels.[17]

Subsequently, while at home Augusto orders large quantities of food from his servant, Liduvina, and starts devouring it voraciously. As he eats, he comes to the realization of *Edo, ergo sum* ("I eat therefore I am") and symbolically this signifies Augusto's hunger for existence. This becomes explicit if we refer again to *The Tragic Sense of Life*, for Unamuno states that a "concrete man" or a "man of flesh and blood" is one who "eats and drinks" and above all "dies." After Augusto finishes devouring these huge meals, he writes Unamuno a telegram to explain that everything has turned out as planned; Augusto undresses, gets into bed and dies. The doctor is summoned to diagnose the case and says Augusto died of a cardiac arrest, but Liduvina says Augusto's problems and eventual death stemmed from his head and the crazy things he was thinking about concerning his existence. But the struggle between the head and heart goes on for the other characters caught up in an absurd existence. The cycle repeats itself for they cannot truly experience their mortality through Augusto's death.

While Liduvina's point acknowledges the limit of reason, it ignores the undeniable yearning of Augusto's heart to endure beyond death. Unamuno seems to say this: can the emotional yearning of the heart towards immortality be reconciled with its rational denial? Unamuno, in this "nivola," says "no" because the head and the heart, by their very nature, are at odds; therefore, it is absurd to believe in immortality. In words Unamuno might have used, Camus says: "This very heart which is mine will forever remain indefinable to me" (*Myth* 19). Yet must one relinquish this hunger for eternal life? Unamuno says "no" once again because the absurd must always be confronted. In other words, the quest for immortality should be insisted upon emphatically because it is unfair for us to be placed into existence and then eliminated, especially since life is so mysterious and alluring that it kindles our passions into demanding more. But as hopeless as our passions may be, we also possess a creativity whereby we can reach out to others and attain a partial immortality. Camus explains that art, as he conceives it, is an opportunity for a person to keep consciousness alive and to give permanence to life's adventures. "Creating is living doubly" (*Myth* 94). And what is to live doubly but a demand for more life: a desire for immortality.

In comparison to Camus and his experiences and consequences of the absurd, Unamuno's legacy is one of passion: to break the tedium of mechanical living through creation; and one of revolt: to proclaim the rational injustice of mortality.

In contrast to the above, one of Camus's consequences of the absurd still remains to be explained: freedom. It is logical to assume that by combining Unamuno's revolt against death and passion for a creative life, both his revolt and passion point to his freedom. The intensity of Unamuno's will to live eternally is his freedom, and it becomes manifest under any absurd circumstances that limit him and, at the same time, excite his will to more life. Looking at *Mist* in its entirety, the consequence of absurd freedom is inherently immanent because Augusto can be directly linked to Sisyphus. Through a simple matter of name substitution—substituting Augusto's name for Sisyphus and Unamuno's name for gods—Unamuno's final goal in *Mist* can be made clearer:

You have already grasped that Sisyphus is the absurd hero. He *is*, as much through his passions as through his torture. His scorn of the gods, his hatred of death, and his passion for life won him that unspeakable penalty in which the whole being is exerted toward accomplishing nothing. (*Myth* 120)

28

NOTES

Alfred Stern, *Sartre: His Philosophy and Existential Psychoanalysis* (New York: Dell Publishing Co., 1967) 3-6.

2 Robert Olson, *An Introduction to Existentialism* (New York: Dover Publications Inc., 1962) 2.

3 Miguel de Unamuno, *The Tragic Sense of Life*, trans. Anthony Kerrigan (Princeton: Princeton UP, 1972) 41.

4 Donald Shaw, *The Generation of 1898* (New York: Barnes and Noble, 1975) 43.

5 Alfred Stern, "Unamuno: Pioneer of Existentialism," *Unamuno: Creator and Creation*, ed. J. R. Barcia and M. A. Zeitlin (Los Angeles and Berkeley: U of Calif. P, 1967) 38.

6 Margaret Rudd, *The Lone Heretic* (New York: Gordian P, 1976) 318-19.

7 Salvador de Madariaga, introduction, *The Tragic Sense of Life*, by Miguel de Unamuno (Princeton: Princeton UP, 1972) xxxii.

8 Albert Camus, *The Myth of Sisyphus and Other Essays*, trans. Justin O'Brien (New York: Alfred Knopf, 1975) 50.

9 Miguel de Unamuno, *How to Make a Novel, Novela/Nivola*, trans. Anthony Kerrigan (Princeton: Princeton UP, 1976) 471.

10 Leon Livingstone, "The Novel as Self-Creation," *Unamuno: Creator and Creation*, ed. J. R. Barcia and M. A. Zeitlin (Los Angeles and Berkeley: U of Calif. P, 1967) 112.

11 Julian Marias, *Miguel de Unamuno*, trans. Frances Lopez-Morillas (Cambridge, Mass.: Harvard UP, 1966) 25.

12 Miguel de Unamuno, *Mist, Novela/Nivola*, trans. Anthony Kerrigan (Princeton: Princeton UP, 1976) 215. In further references to this work in CHAPTER II, I will use page numbers only.

NOTES

[13] Jean-Paul Sartre, "The Humanism of Existentialism," *Essays in Existentialism*, ed. Wade Baskin (Secaucus, N. J. : Citadel Press, 1965) 56.

[14] Frances Weber, "Unamuno's *Niebla*: From Novel to Dream," *PMLA* 87 (1973): 209.

[15] Sören Kierkegaard, "Truth Is Subjectivity," *Existentialism from Dostoevsky to Sartre*, ed. Walter Kaufmann (New York: New American Library, 1975) 110.

[16] On this point see my discussion in Chapter III concerning practical jokes, laughter, and the comic.

[17] Alexander Parker, "On the Interpretation of *Niebla*," *Unamuno: Creator and Creation*, ed. J. R. Barcia and M. A. Zeitlin (Los Angeles and Berkeley: U of Calif. P, 1967) 135.

CHAPTER III

NAUSEA

Of all the existentialist writers I shall consider in this book, Jean-Paul Sartre is certainly one of the most prolific. Besides being a dramatist, a social commentator, a literary critic, and a novelist, Sartre is also an astute philosopher. My intent in this chapter is to explore Sartre's use of the absurd, first in his philosophy and then in his fiction, while comparing his view to that of Camus.

As I stated in the previous chapter, the one defining feature of existentialism that all existentialists would agree upon is the idea that "existence precedes essence." In Sartre's essay "The Humanism of Existentialism," he states his philosophical position on existentialism:

> Atheistic existentialism, which I represent, is more coherent. It states that if God does not exist, there is at least one being in whom existence precedes essence, a being who exists before he can be defined by any concept, and that being is man or, as Heidegger says, human reality. What is meant here by saying that existence precedes essence? It means first of all, man exists, turns up, appears on the scene, and, only afterwards, defines himself. If man, as the existentialist conceives him, is indefinable, it is because at first he is nothing. Only afterward will he be something, and he himself will have made what he will be.[1]

The question of being, for Sartre, is studied from a subjective vantage point, and, like Unamuno, there is a change from the primacy of knowledge to the primacy of existence. Hence Sartre wanted a shift from epistemology to ontology. Sartre's existentialist ontology studies the structures of being and describes the "what" and the "how" (rather than the "why") of human reality as it manifests itself in the world. Yet how did he figure this out? A phenomenological description is offered by Luther Binkley:

> The subtitle of *Being and Nothingness* is *An Essay on Phenomenological Ontology*. This rather forbidding phrase indicates that Sartre's objective in this book is to describe the basic structures of the world and of man in terms of the way these structures actually appear to us in our experience.[2]

Sartre was critical of traditional philosophy; for instance, he rejected the Kantian separation of noumena and phenomena, which designated our world as the appearance of a reality which was—in itself—inaccessible to us. According to Kant, the noumenal world (things in themselves) was beyond our reach because the phenomenal world is the only world we can know.[3] Sartre took exception to this and adopted Hegel's terms of being-in-itself (*l'être-en-soi*) and being-for-itself (*l'être-pour-soi*) to distinguish non-conscious from conscious entities.[4] Sartre described inanimate objects as in-itself, that is, objects which are self-identical; such objects do not question themselves. However, we can determine the essence of an in-itself object, but its being is transphenomenal; its being overflows its essence.

On the other hand, there is being-for-itself, which is what Sartre calls the individual consciousness. Since consciousness is for-itself (does not have the self-identity of the in-itself) it is described by Sartre as a lack, or emptiness, an ability to found its own "nothingness" of being.[5] The for-itself contrasts with the in-itself (which simply "is") because the for-itself is always in a constant process of becoming.

All of Sartre's ontology, therefore, revolves around the in-itself and the for-itself. Sartre's analysis of these two antithetical properties indicates that being in-itself is given to the for-itself through the experience of nausea and the absurd: "To human consciousness, being-in-itself is absurd, disgusting, nauseating" (Binkley 170). Therefore, the in-itself is transphenomenal because it overflows our knowledge of things, and we know it through emotional apprehension. Camus concurs with this view of the split between ourselves and objects and also relates this experience to the absurd when he states in *The Myth of Sisyphus*:

> A step lower and strangeness creeps in: perceiving that the
> world is "dense," sensing to what a degree a stone is foreign
> and irreducible to us, with what intensity nature or a landscape
> can negate us. [...] Just one thing: that denseness and that
> strangeness of the world is the absurd. [6]

Being just "is"—there is no reason for it—that is the sense of the absurd
which relates to the feeling of nausea and to two other antithetical properties
which characterize human beings in the world: facticity and transcendence.

Our existence is given to us through the pre-reflective *cogito*. It is also
transphenomenal (a transcendence): it goes beyond what we can know, but
we can have conscious awareness of it: "Just as my nihilating freedom is ap-
prehended in anguish, so the for-itself is conscious of its facticity. It has the
feeling of its complete gratuity; it apprehends itself as being there *for nothing*, as being *de trop*" (Sartre, *Being* 84). In the chapter on "The Body" in
Being and Nothingness, Sartre also states:

> What for the Other is his *taste of himself* becomes for me the
> Other's *flesh*. The flesh is the pure contingency of presence. It
> is ordinarily hidden by clothes, make-up, the cut of the hair or
> beard, the expression, etc. But in the course of long acquain-
> tance with a person there always comes an instant when all
> these disguises are thrown off and when I find myself in the
> presence of the pure *contingency of his presence*. In this case I
> achieve in the face or the other parts of a body the pure intuition
> of flesh. This intuition is not only knowledge; it is the affective
> apprehension of an absolute contingency, and this apprehension
> is a particular type of *nausea*. (343-44)

The absolute contingency (our lack of necessity because of our facticity) that
Sartre describes here is another expression of the absurd and is thus highly
pertinent to my discussion.

In *The Myth of Sisyphus* (15), Camus makes direct reference to Sartre and
this experience of the absurd when he states: "This discomfort in the face of
man's own inhumanity, this incalculable tumble before the image of what we
are, this 'nausea,' as a writer of today calls it, is also the absurd." Sartre and
Camus want to put the person as subject into the center of their philosophical
discussion, which is to say they both sought to understand and interpret
human behavior and experience. In this context, both men make reference to
the experience of nausea as an absurd awareness of existence: we exist in the

world, we are present to others, and nausea is an access to our existence.

In short, this gap of nothingness between a person (the for-itself) and the world (the in-itself) is part of the absurd. H. Gene Blocker explains: "In the first sense nothingness is the gap between man and the world (consciousness and what we are conscious of) which, in our discussion, is simply another name for absurdity it its simplest form" (53). He further states:

> It is the perception of this split that accounts for the experience of absurdity and nausea [...]. In *Being and Nothingness* this experience which Sartre calls "nausea" is limited to my experience of my own body as an alien being-in-itself, threatening, negating my self, my consciousness for-itself. But it is threatening not only in the sense that it reveals how I am not, but in the more primitive sense [...] that I depend on this body, however different I am from it internally, and that my very being is at the mercy of something totally alien from me. (68-69)

Therefore, it is this distinct rift between ourselves and the objects in the world, and the rift between ourselves and our bodies, which is manifest in the experience of the absurd. It is these two experiences of the absurd which brings Sartre and Camus together, but the question of method now arises.

In *What is Literature?* Sartre states:

> The "engaged" writer knows that words are action. He knows that to reveal is to change and that one can reveal only by planning to change. He has given up the impossible dream of giving an impartial picture of Society and the human condition. [...] [W]e may conclude that the writer has chosen to reveal the world and particularly to reveal man to other men so that the latter may assume full responsibility before the object which has been thus laid bare.[7]

In view of these statements one might ask: what methods will the engaged writer use to reveal a person and the world? A safe generalization to make which concerns Sartre as one of the best representatives of the existentialists is to say that he experimented with different literary methods to make his point. Although philosophical essays and drama were part of his repertoire, it was his fictional work that cogently demonstrated his philosophical position in a human setting and made his work more appealing and accessible to the world: "One of the chief motives of artistic creation is certainly the need of feeling that we are essential in relationship to the world" (Sartre, *What* 39).

This diversity in the arts, which Sartre explored by writing fiction, proves viable for him because he did not want to isolate himself in a particular genre in order to describe our being-in-the-world. The novel for Sartre provides an object/subject setting: objective because everyone has the ability to experience what he presents, subjective because each individual chooses that which is appropriate to his or her needs. By using the novel as an art form, Sartre is reacting against the traditional philosophical belief that any emphasis on individual, creative experience is for artists, not philosophers. To counteract this, Sartre documented his changes from traditional philosophy through fiction, so as not to lose touch with human experience.

Sartre especially wanted to write what he called "the literature of great circumstance." The most profound idea concerning this literature is what he termed the "literature of praxis"—praxis meaning action.[8] In this way the ordinary means of presenting traditional philosophical methods are circumvented, which seemed remote from life since they are very abstract. Fiction is used to give some examples of his basic philosophical posture: to promote more readily the principles of our commitment to responsibility, freedom, and engagement.

Given the above, Sartre's novel *Nausea* may be studied from the point of view of the absurd since he focuses upon this experience in that work. In words that could very well describe *Nausea* and Sartre's attempt at creating fiction, Camus says in relationship to novelists and the absurd:

> The essential is that the novelists should triumph in the concrete and that this constitute their nobility. This wholly carnal triumph has been prepared for them by a thought in which abstract powers have been humiliated. When they are completely so, at the same time the flesh makes creation shine forth in all its absurd luster. (*Myth* 116)

Of Sartre's novels, *Nausea* (1938) is the one that is critically acclaimed as his best, in part because it stresses the absurdity of contingency. Briefly stated, the novel purports to be an intimate diary kept by a certain Antoine Roquentin; he is a world traveler who settles down in Bouville (Mudtown) in order to write about the Marquis de Rollebon, an historical figure who was prominent in France's history. The main theme of the novel, as the title indicates, is that Roquentin keeps experiencing nausea as he picks up or perceives objects in the world:

> Now I see: I recall better what I felt the other day at the
> seashore when I held the pebble. It was a sort of sweetish sick-
> ness. How unpleasant it was! It came from the stone, I'm sure
> of it, it passed from the stone to my hand. Yes that's it, that's
> just it—a sort of nausea in the hands.[9]

To cure his nausea, Roquentin immerses himself in the past and tries to
have vicarious adventures by reading books and writing a historical biography, and this seems to provide a partial respite to his nausea. The ontological
contingency of Roquentin's being-in-the-world can be understood in successive layers and as each layer is pulled back, the absurd becomes increasingly
manifest. The first layer is the clash between a knowing consciousness and
the opaque (objects known in the world). This outer layer of the absurd is
described in Roquentin's diary: the rift between himself (knowledge) and
objects (reality). Searching his memory and examining his past, Roquentin
attempts to record what is happening to him:

> The best thing would be to write down events from day to day.
> Keep a diary to see clearly—let none of the nuances or small
> happenings escape even though they might seem to mean noth-
> ing. And above all, classify them. I must tell how I see this
> table, this street, the people, my packet of tobacco, since those
> are the things which have changed. I must determine the exact
> extent and nature of this change. (1)

Of course, it is not the objects which have changed, but it is Roquentin's
perception of them. In this outer layer of the absurd, the mere fact of writing,
of labeling things, indicates that the label he gives an object describes only
its essence (certain characteristics which distinguish the object from other
objects). But there is a rift between labels, descriptions, and explanations, on
the one hand, and the brute existence of things on the other:

> Everywhere, now, there are objects like this glass of beer on the
> table there. When I see it, I feel like saying: "Enough." I realize
> quite well that I have gone too far. [...] I have been *avoiding*
> looking at this glass of beer for half an hour. [...] It's just like all
> the others. It's bevelled on the edges, has a handle, a little coat
> of arms with a spade on it and on the coat of arms is written
> "Spartenbrau," I know all that, but I know there is something
> else. Almost nothing. But I can't explain what I see. (8)

Early in the story, it becomes evident that the nausea he experiences comes from the revelation of the sheer existence of things:

> His blue cotton shirt stands out joyfully against a chocolate-coloured wall. That too brings on the Nausea. The Nausea is not inside me: I feel it *out there* in the wall, in the suspenders, everywhere around me. It makes itself one with the café, I am the one who is within *it*. (19-20)

As stated earlier, the in-itself (brute existence) cannot be fully explained by the for-itself (human consciousness), and we can see Roquentin's frustration in attempting to articulate what is "absurd," without any given meaning. He knows objects exist, but it makes no sense to ask what they are or what they mean: "For instance, here is a cardboard box holding my bottle of ink. I should try to tell how I saw it *before* and now how I [see it]. Well, it's a parallelopiped rectangle, it opens—that's stupid, there's nothing I can say about it" (1).

As the story unfolds, there are various instances in which Roquentin sees familiar objects differently, and it loosens his tentative hold on existence. The work of memory, which gives objects meaning and coherence, breaks down for Roquentin, and he must simply rely on what he can see or touch. Through Roquentin's experience of riding on the tramway, we see the absurd manifest in the clash between existence and essence. The nauseous description of a seat as a bloated, dead donkey is an ironic attempt to describe existence; but it is at the same time a refutation that any such description is fully possible, since existence is a plenitude, an overflowing. Sartre is attempting to intensify the rift between the word (a description of the for-itself/a human construct) and the object (the opaque in-itself). Human perception in its confrontation with brute existence, stripped of its human meaning, reveals that the world is indifferent to our labels and has a density and existence of its own, exclusive of how we label it or use it. The in-itself simply *is*:

> I lean my hand on the seat but pull it back hurriedly: it exists. This thing I'm sitting on, leaning my hand on, is called a seat. They made it purposely for people to sit on, they took leather, springs and cloth, they went to work with the idea of making a seat and when they finished, *that* was what they had made. They carried it here, into this car and the car is now rolling and jolting with its rattling windows, carrying this red thing in its

bosom. I murmur: "it's a seat," a little like an exorcism. But the word stays on my lips: it refuses to go and put itself on the thing. It stays what it is, with its red plush, thousands of little red paws in the air, all still, little dead paws. This enormous belly turned upward, bleeding, inflated—bloated with all its dead paws, this belly floating in this car, in this grey sky, is not a seat. It could just as well be a dead donkey tossed about in the water, floating with the current, belly in the air in a great grey river, a river of floods; and I could be sitting on the donkey's belly, my feet dangling in the clear water. Things are divorced from their names. They are there, grotesque, headstrong, gigantic and it seems ridiculous to call them seats or say anything at all about them: I am in the midst of things, nameless things. Alone, without words, defenceless, they surround me, are beneath me, behind me, above me. They demand nothing, they don't impose themselves: they are there. (125)

In the experience of nausea, objects lose their labels; labels no longer attach themselves to their objects. Divorced from one another both word and object take on a peculiar denseness and foreignness. The experience of nausea is an experience of the absurd, a realization that labels, descriptions and the like are human constructs and have nothing to do with existence, but merely serve our practical purposes. Colin Wilson, a critic of existentialist literature, summarizes this attitude: "Roquentin feels insignificant before things. Without the meaning his Will would normally impose on it, his existence is absurd."[10]

Inevitably, Roquentin begins to understand that the past, which he has tried to recapture through his reading, has blinded him as to the lack of meaning or purpose in his life:

M. de Rollebon was my partner; he needed me in order to exist and I needed him so as not to feel my existence. I furnished the raw material, the material I had to re-sell, which I didn't know what to do with: existence, *my* existence. His part was to have an imposing appearance. He stood in front of me, took up my life *to lay* bare his own to me. I did not notice that I existed any more, I no longer existed in myself, but in him [...]. I was only a means of making him live, he was my reason for living, he had delivered me from myself. What shall I do now? (98)

Roquentin's existence can now be understood from the next layer of the absurd: the rift between the for-itself (our present intent) and the in-itself (the past and our future possibilities). We are beings in the world who make our own rules, yet we can only realize ourselves by finding our values outside of ourselves. In other words, we make our choices (values) by ourselves, and this is our responsibility; also we are responsible for our actions in the future because our values come from our future projects, which are present projections. "We should note that, in a sense, both the present and the future are 'future,' for they are both flights from being toward a beyond" (Catalano 118). Second, we are also outside of ourselves in that we are the sum total of the choices we have made in life (our past); therefore, we impress our being on the external world and find outside of ourselves particular transcendent goals. So it seems that we are our past and future selves and this is our responsibility, yet we are not identical with our past and future selves. As temporal process, we are always becoming who we are—hence we are condemned to freedom. "We have to deal with human reality as a being which is what it is not and which is not what it is" (Sartre, *Essays* 165). Hazel Barnes explains this radical freedom:

> That man is free and self-transcending, and that there is no determining human nature are empty mouthings of dogma unless we believe that man has the possibility of becoming something quite different from what he has been—and this existentially, not just socially and technologically. To say that he *will* do so is to make a statement of faith, not merely to hazard a guess as to whether man will or will not live up to his potentialities.[11]

If we try to forget about our contingency (our gratuitousness or our lack of necessity), we are in bad faith. This may take the form of an escape, which must end in failure. This is where the experience of nausea, trying to experience the past, and the consequence of freedom overlap. For example, Roquentin is constantly trying to recapture the past (escape into it) through his historical reading because he feels abandoned in the present. Although the past is no longer real, he thinks that the recollection of it will help him relive it; and it will give some type of meaning to his life: he seeks events which he may call "adventures." He seeks some adventures, so he can forget about his contingency; but the adventures he has experienced have only been in books: "It seems as though I have learned all I know of life in books" (64). As all of Roquentin's past meanings break down, he becomes limited to the present. This is the nausea that characterizes the present for Roquentin

because the feeling of adventure and the feeling of nausea are opposites, and
he sought adventure in order to escape the nausea:

> Nothing has changed and yet everything is different. I can't de-
> scribe it; it's like the Nausea and yet it's just the opposite: at
> last an adventure happens to me and when I question myself I
> see that it happens *that I am myself and that I am here.* (54)

He is discovering that the past, since he is trying to recapture it in the present, can never exist again exactly as it was; he must determine the past's
meaning in view of the present:

> I am beginning to believe that nothing can ever be proved.
> These are honest hypotheses which take the facts into account;
> but I sense so definitely that they come from me, and that they
> are simply a way of unifying my own knowledge. [...] Slow,
> lazy, sulky, the facts adapt themselves to the rigour of the order
> I wish to give them; but it remains outside of them. (13)

Like the nausea that comes and goes, so do the adventures:

> Perhaps there is nothing in the world I cling to as much as this
> feeling of adventure; but it comes when it pleases; it is gone so
> quickly and how empty I am once it has left. Does it, ironically,
> pay me these short visits in order to show me that I have wasted
> my life? (56)

Once Roquentin learns he *is* nausea, then he understands that there are no
real adventures since the two are opposites and yet related: nausea is not
something he can learn to stay away from, and, inversely, adventures are not
something he can go out and find. Roquentin is free—ontologically contingent—and any attempt to escape from his present contingency must end in
failure. Camus explains this absurd freedom in terms of the present too:
"This hell of the present is his Kingdom at last" (*Myth* 52).

Roquentin's relationship with his former mistress, Anny, can also be
viewed in these terms. After a long separation, the two finally meet again; he
finds that she has given up her search for "perfect moments"; she contents
herself with being kept by another man, so she can merely exist in the past:
"I live in the past. I take everything that has happened to me and arrange it.
From a distance like that, it doesn't do any harm, you'd almost let yourself

be caught in it" (152). Anny also wants to fix Roquentin's present existence in the past, so she can treat him as an object: "I need you to exist and not to change. You're like that platinum wire they keep in Paris or somewhere in the neighborhood. I don't think anyone's ever needed to see it" (137). He also finds out that any adventures he did have with Anny were constructs by her in her attempt to create "perfect moments." Both have been traveling a similar route, though separately, these last years; she too has been reading books, Michelet's *History of France*, in order to give her life a vicarious purpose in the past: "That's it. There are no adventures—there are no perfect moments...we have lost the same illusions, we have followed the same paths. I can guess the rest—I can even speak for her and tell myself all that she has left to tell" (150).

The futility of trying to find some sort of meaning in his adventures is a cogent reminder that the past is dead. Roquentin presently knows that there are no adventures in life other than what you make of them. Adventures are something he has made up in his mind, a linking up of events, in order to give him a sense of drama. The events themselves have no relationship to one another, but he has attempted to give them some sort of relationship:

> This feeling of adventure definitely does not come from events: I have proved it. It's rather the way in which the moments are linked together. I think this is what happens: you suddenly feel that time is passing, that each instant leads to another, this one to another one, and so on; that each instant is annihilated, and that it isn't worth while to hold it back [...]. You talk a lot about this amazing flow of time but you hardly see it. You see a woman, you think that one day she'll be old, only you don't see her grow old. But there are moments when you think you *see* her grow old and feel yourself growing old with her: this is the feeling of adventure. (56-57)

How has Roquentin realized that adventures do not come from events? It is another one of Camus's experiences of the absurd: time passing, relating to the experience of nausea: "He belongs to time, and by the horror that seizes him, he recognizes his worst enemy [...]. That revolt of the flesh is the absurd" (*Myth* 14). At first Roquentin notices the citizens of Bouville and how they experience the fleetingness of the present moment as they stroll on the beach on a Sunday afternoon: "They felt the minutes flowing between their fingers; would they have enough time to store up enough youth to start anew on Monday morning" (52)? Finally they return home and "Sunday has left them with a taste of ashes and their thoughts are already turning towards Monday" (54). Later he relates this to his past relationship with Anny, growing old with her, and his revelation that there are no perfect moments or adventures. In Roquentin's notion of adventure there remains the irreversibility of time. Once again the nausea sets in to confirm this: "I have plunged into her strange universe, beyond ridicule, affectation, subtlety. I have even recovered the little fever that always stirred in me when I was with her, and this bitter taste in the back of my mouth" (144).

However, to counteract this contingency of being-in-the-world, Roquentin likes to listen to the song "Some of These Days" at one of the bars he frequents, the Railwaymen's Rendezvous, to describe how he can be at ease in the world—remember the past in terms of the present—and overcome his nausea: "What has just happened is that the Nausea has disappeared. When the voice was heard in the silence, I felt my body harden and the Nausea vanish" (22). As his nausea disappears, objects resume their customary shape for him: his glass of beer apparently reduces to normal size, and "both his own gestures and those of the card-players at the table next to him become harmonious and meaningful."[12] Not only does the music help him to overcome his nausea, but it helps him to annihilate the passage of time: "At the same time the music was drawn out, dilated, swelled like a waterspout. It filled the room with its metallic transparency, crushing our miserable time against the walls" (22). Roquentin is now content: "I grow warm, I begin to feel happy. There is nothing extraordinary in this, it is a small happiness of Nausea" (21). The conclusion here is illuminated for us in a human setting: the past can only exist insofar as he chooses to determine the present meaning of past events. In this instance possibilities arise for him when he projects his being into the future. Roquentin can only realize who he is by finding outside of himself the paths which lead to his freedom.

In retrospect, Roquentin has been using his past relationship with Anny and his historical reading as an escape from the world and the absurd, rather than confronting it: "You don't put your past in your pocket; you have to have a house. I have only my body: a man entirely alone, with his lonely body, cannot indulge in memories; they pass through him. I shouldn't complain: all I wanted was to be free" (65). Subsequently, the nausea he experiences brings him back to reality and he starts to realize his contingency. Contingency in this instance means absurdity.[13] This idea of recognizing the absurd, leading to the knowledge of contingency, is the final layer that must be peeled back to reveal the inner layer: the absurd rift between facticity and transcendence.

At the end of the novel in the park scene, the nausea he continually experiences enables him to understand his existence: he *is* nausea. Nausea is the physical feeling which tells his consciousness that he is his body; therefore, Roquentin comes to the revelation in the park that life is essentially absurd and he is *de trop* (unnecessary) unless he seizes control of his life and moves forward. This means the world offers no higher meaning, and he must create his own. So he concludes he will move out of Bouville and write a novel. This is actually a method Sartre uses to convey his ideas about our contingency (lack of necessity) and our passion for life in relationship to two antithetical human properties: facticity (our being-in-the-world which includes our bodies, birth, class, education, and past) and transcendence (our projection of ourselves into the future), which also gives us our meaning and values. Our passion for life consists in transcending our facticity towards goals we have personally chosen—our essence is our past and we are what we have made ourselves.

In light of these summary remarks, the key to *Nausea*, as most critics observe,[14] is Roquentin's epiphany in the park. However, most critics overlook the humor that is present here. If I scrutinize this episode, concerning Roquentin's reflections about the comic and vaudeville, I can try to formulate a different hypothesis of how Roquentin comes to his revelation in the park in relationship to the absurd.

Briefly stated, Roquentin goes to the park, sits on a bench, and looks at the roots of a chestnut tree. He has a vision: existence unveils itself. The root of the tree is the very "past of existence" or it is "kneaded into existence"; then everything he observes melts away (objects in the world become a veneer) leaving "soft monstrous masses." In the same way that Roquentin feels his own existence as nauseating and inescapable, he also makes a similar discovery concerning objects: they are simply there "in the way" like him with no reason for being. Directly afterwards Roquentin hears a fountain bubbling and thinks to himself that all things let themselves drift into existence like "those relaxed women who burst out laughing and say: 'It's good to laugh'" (128). Here Roquentin begins to understand the distinction between facticity and transcendence and thinks that there is no half-way point between non-existence and abundance: if you existed, you must exist completely; but "existence is a deflection." Next, he thinks of the fountain as bubbling "happily" and thinks of himself digesting a meal on a park bench; he reflects that all these meals digested together have their comic side (this is analogous to the *Edo, ergo sum* credo of the protagonist in Unamuno's *Mist*). Yet he thinks that it doesn't go as far as this, and he qualifies himself by stating that existence is like a floating analogy, with certain aspects of vaudeville. Obviously, he concludes that no object in the world is comic in itself, for it is the subjective attitude that one takes toward the object which makes it comic. Directly after this explanation of existence and the comic, Roquentin thinks that the world is absurd, and this makes him feel contingent and "in the way" (*de trop*). Finally, Roquentin understands his existence because it is absurd: "I understand that I had found the key to Existence, the key to my Nauseas, to my own life. In fact, all that I could grasp beyond that returns to this fundamental absurdity" (129). Later he reflects about the trees again, and since trees are an abundance, "great clumsy bodies," he begins to laugh. He thinks of those "idiots who come to tell you about "will-power" and the "struggle for life," and he wonders if they have ever seen a tree. Finally, he leaves the park and glances back at the garden and the trees smile at him. He knows that the smile of the trees meant something, and that was the "real secret of existence."

What does the smile of the trees signify? Could it possibly be the curling of one's lips before laughter? From a humorous standpoint Roquentin's discussion of existence as a "floating analogy" to vaudeville becomes apparent because an analogy is an extended metaphor or simile to persuade the reader that because two things are alike, a conclusion from one suggests a conclusion from the other. And what is vaudeville but a "light" often "comic" theatrical performance by people in which they combine dancing, song, dialogue, or pantomime. Here is the analogy: the comic is to vaudeville as Roquentin's absurdity is to his existence; therefore, the comic and the absurd are aspects of something transcendent, the human passion for more life.

Roquentin's revelation is the realization that human existence is absurd, because the absurd, by any common definition of the word, means incongruity, which is also the key to most of the modern definitions of humor. It is also analogous to Camus's definition of the absurd. Wylie Sypher makes this especially evident in one of his essays by saying that the absurd is comic and is also one of the cornerstones of existentialism.[15] Max Eastman, in *Sense of Humor*, also states that the absurd is the best name we can choose for humor.[16] Yet the best evidence that this is true comes from Sartre himself in one of his later works *The Family Idiot*. In the section on the practical joke, Sartre says that when familiar objects become suspect, then the world takes on a strange dimension (much like Roquentin and his revelation while in the park). Sartre goes on to explain that the practical joke evokes this type of "estrangement" as one relates to the world because the world is allergic to people. Sartre uses the fake sugar cube as an example which is in reality a piece of marble or a celluloid cube. As the unknowing person weighs the sugar cube in his or her hand and it seems heavy or it floats on top in the coffee cup, the world becomes dense and foreign: one cannot rely on anything. In words similar to those Camus used in *The Myth of Sisyphus* to describe the incommensurability between nature and humans, Sartre says: "*I don't believe my eyes*, I seem a stranger to myself, my habits are disqualified, my past abolished; I am naked in a new present that is lost in an unknown future."[17] The practical joker who offered the sugar cube is aware of the feelings of the one who is duped precisely "for the perfectly good reason that he has often felt it himself" and "the joke is a demonstration by absurdity of [...] the permanence of the laws of nature" (*Idiot* 205-06). If the joke is successful and the one who is duped laughs with the joker, the practical joke becomes a kind of innoculation against the world. This ridiculous laughter makes us aware of our existence through the self-realization of our contingency. In volume two of *The Family Idiot* Sartre also says that

> "laughter, though born of fear, is accompanied by intense pleasure[...]. [B]oth contagious and willed, it comes to me *through the other* and has taken hold of my body, meaning that it *has chosen me*; I have not produced it, I have submitted to it and adhered to it—it is proof that I have all the qualities of a man. (*Idiot* 165-66)

In other words, people laugh when they radically perceive incongrouous ideas, situations, events, or people, and one possible indication of this absurd perception is laughter, which demonstrates passion. Once Roquentin realizes this, his heart is moved and things begin to float because he now realizes he is free: "All is free, this park, this city, and myself. When you realized that, it turns your heart upside down and everything beings to float" (131).

This comic awareness of his passion enables Roquentin to float on the waves of things, and this draws him out of his nausea. Humorous laughter, the kind that Roquentin and the women in the park are displaying, is a unique quality of feeling because it is part of what we do in life; it is a passionate action which has significance: it is evident that Roquentin has formerly lived only through a rational awareness of life, denying his passion. According to Sartre, we are composed of certain antithetical properties that create a dynamic tension in us, or, once again, "We have to deal with human reality as a being which is what it is not and which is not what it is." What separates the nausea from laughter is the nothingness, which, according to Sartre, "lies coiled in the heart of being—like a worm" (*Being* 21). This nothingness is our consciousness which affects itself with passion; Roquentin learns this, laughs, and the trees smile at him in return. The smile of the trees is a metaphor indicating Roquentin's comic self-realization that he is not simply a thinking, nauseous body, but a free-feeling and passionate individual. This is implicit in the statement "when you realize that, it turns your heart upside down and everything begins to float," which also implies the comical lightness of theatrical performances in vaudeville and successful practical jokes (floating sugar cube or not). Also implicit in this statement is the clash between his head and his heart, also creating the absurd, as I argued in my discussion of Unamuno.

Sartre summarizes life toward the end of *Being and Nothingness* by saying, "man is a useless passion." In relationship to *Nausea*, people are useless passions who attempt to deny their contingency and assert their sacred rights. On this point Sartre is adamant because there is no choice for contingency. One can only be contingent and know it or be contingent and hide it from oneself (live in bad faith). Roquentin states: "Every existing thing is born without reason, prolongs itself out of weakness and dies by chance" (133). The people who live in bad faith are *salauds* (the skunks or bastards) who claim sacred rights and refuse their contingency:

> The essential thing is contingency. I mean that one cannot define existence as necessity. To exist is simply *to be there*; those who exist let themselves be encountered, but you can never deduce anything from them. I believe there are people who have understood this. Only they have tried to overcome this contingency by inventing a necessary, causal being. But no necessary being can explain existence; contingency is not a delusion, a probability which can be dissipated; it is the absolute, consequently, the perfect free gift. [...] [H]ere is Nausea; here there is what those bastards [...] try to hide from themselves with their idea of rights. But what a poor lie: no one has any rights; they are entirely free, like other men, they cannot succeed in not feeling *superfluous*. (131)

In contrast, people are good passions who confront the absurd and acknowledge their contingency, by recognizing their freedom and passions, and revolting against past, accepted, ready-made values and knowledge. Camus explains passion as one of the consequences of the absurd, and in many respects, addresses in a positive way Sartre's statement concerning humans as useless passions:

> But what does life mean in such a universe? Nothing else for the moment but indifference to the future and a desire to use up

everything that is given. Belief in the meaning of life always
implies a scale of values, a choice, our preference. Belief in the
absurd, according to our definitions, teaches the contrary. (*Myth*
60)

Since Roquentin's life is absurd and his existence is unnecessary, yet he
does exist, he concludes that life is an absolute—a free gift. Roquentin is
discovering, through these successive layers of the absurd that must be
stripped back, that he does not know everything, nor *can* he know everything: "I wanted to peel off some of the bark. For no reason at all, out of defiance, to make the bare pink appear absurd on the tanned leather: to *play*
with the absurdity of the world" (130). Roquentin finally learns that the
world of definitions and reason is not "the world of existence" because it
denies one's passions and feelings. It is out of this passion for more life,
against this world of human rationality, that Roquentin wants to impose his
absurd being. He realizes that those who try to overcome their contingency
are living in bad faith because everyone is radically free. In contrast to the
beginning of the story when Roquentin states that his "passion" is "dead," he
now has a passion for maximum living. All Roquentin has really wanted was
this, *to be*:

And I too, want to *be*. That is all I wanted; this is the last word.
At the bottom of all these attempts which seemed without
bonds, I find the same desire again: to drive existence out of
me, to rid the passing moments of their fat, to twist them, dry
them, purify myself, harden myself, to give back at last the
sharp, precise sound of a saxophone note. (175)

At the end of *Nausea*, Roquentin has determined that the world is engulf-
ing him, and he makes three important decisions: to move out of Bouville, to
stop writing his historical book of Rollebon, to write a novel instead. These
decisions sum up the three layers of the absurd I have described in terms of
revolt, freedom, and passion.

First, his decision to move out of Bouville is significant in terms of revolt. He will move to Paris and recreate his life, trying to have a fuller com-
mand of his being. Out of "nothingness" he will revolt against the ready-
made meanings and definitions that the established society of Bouville has
tried to instill in him. The satiric sketch of Bouville's museum, with the por-
traits of yesterday's leading citizens—men with self-confident glares looking
down at Roquentin—is especially noteworthy since these men believed their

existence necessary. Roquentin states: "Farewell, beautiful lilies, elegant in your painted little sanctuaries, good-bye, lovely lilies, our pride and reason for existing, good-bye you bastards" (94). Through change and fulfillment in another city, he will seek new possibilities (new ways of thinking and feeling), revolting against the *salauds* who permeate this city. Philip Thody explains:

> Beneath the apparent calm of the European society which Bouville reflects in its most stable form, the forces of evil which were to lead, in September 1939, to the outbreak of the World War II, had already begun to make their presence felt. [...] If the inhabitants of Bouville feel reassured at living in a regular universe where "bodies in a vacuum all fall at the same speed, the public garden is closed everyday at four o'clock in winter and at six in summer, lead melts at 338 degrees centigrade, the last tram leaves the Town Hall at five minutes past eleven," then they have made the mistake of confusing regularity with inevitability.[18]

Moreover, the "Self-Taught Man," with his false sense of humanism, whom Roquentin rejects, could very well be another central figure of this decadent city's collapse. The "Self-Taught Man" seeks all the knowledge the town library has to offer (in alphabetical order), but actually contents himself with caressing young school boys who frequent the library. The concluding line of the novel, "tomorrow it will rain in Bouville," suggests some sort of needed purification for this city and the people who inhabit it. In fact, one could say Bouville is "this incalculable tumble before the image of what we are, this 'nausea,' as a writer of today calls it." Roquentin revolts against this provincial and bourgeois city by leaving. He wants to challenge the world anew at every instant; his revolt gives him consciousness in an absurd universe.

Second, Roquentin decides to quit writing the historical biography of Rollebon: "I have made my decision: I have no more reason for staying in Bouville since I'm not writing my book anymore" (135). Roquentin has learned that "an existant can never justify the existence of another existant. My error, I wanted to resuscitate the Marquis de Rollebon" (178). After the revelation in the park, Roquentin knows that he is radically free, and he experiences this freedom, in nausea, as pure contingency, pure absurdity. The information he has on Rollebon's life means nothing in itself. Any of Rollebon's past acts have no meaning except that which, by free imaginative action, Roquentin wishes to bestow upon them. Roquentin's view of the separation of the past from the present is inherent in his absurd freedom to choose.

Finally, as Roquentin is sitting in his usual café, waiting for the train, he hears the lines of his favorite song, "Some of these days, You'll miss me, honey"; the song leads him to believe he should write a novel instead. He understands that the song explains itself, for it is not *de trop*: "It does not exist because it has nothing superfluous: it is all the rest which in relation to it is superfluous. It *is*" (175). The song is the perfect adventure that Roquentin has been seeking all along. Here we see the passion of artistic creation as a consequence of the absurd. The song exists independently of the record on which it is recorded; he knows that he could get up and smash the record, but the melody would continue to exist by itself. But when he hears it, this leads him to remember the Negress who sang it and the Jewish songwriter who wrote it. The song exists independent of them, but there is an artistic connection which brings it into existence, and they were essential to the song: music allows him to confront his nausea because the melody is not contingent. Sartre, like Unamuno, is using art as a means of attaining immortality—that hunger for more life—by confronting his absurd existence. Camus explains once again: "In this universe the work of art is then the sole chance of keeping his consciousness and of fixing its adventures. Creating is living doubly." At the end of the novel, Roquentin's last few statements relate to this passion for more life through artistic creation:

> A story for example, something that could never happen, an adventure. It would have to be beautiful and hard as steel and make people ashamed of their existence. [...] And there would be people who read this book and say: "Antoine Roquentin wrote it, a red-headed man who hung around cafés," and they would think about my life as I think about the Negress's: as something precious and almost legendary. [...] Then, perhaps, because of it, I could remember my life without repugnance. [...] [P]erhaps I shall feel my heart beat faster and say to myself: "That was the day, that was the hour, when it all started." (178)

Art as a means of salvation is inherent in this novel, but Sartre would later refute this idea. Camus, in *The Myth of Sisyphus*, comes closer in defining what artistic creation does in terms of absurdist literature:

> It would be wrong to see a symbol in it and to think that the

work of art can be considered at last as a refuge for the absurd. [...] It does not offer an escape for the intellectual ailment. [...] But for the first time it makes the mind get outside of itself and places it in opposition to others, not for it to get lost but to show it clearly the blind path that all have entered upon. (*Myth* 95)

In light of this passage, *Nausea*, as absurdist literature, is a highly creative novel; it expresses a passion for living and a desire for more life, rejecting any transcendent meanings in life. It is simply one man's search to find some type of personal value through the myriad possibilities that life offers by describing the absurd in concrete human terms.

NOTES

[1] Jean-Paul Sartre, "The Humanism of Existentialism," *Essays in Existentialism*, ed. Wade Baskin (Secaucus, N. J.: Citadel Press, 1965) 35-36.

[2] Luther Binkley, *Conflict of Ideals: Changing Values in Western Society* (New York: Van Nostrand/Reynolds Co., 1969) 166.

[3] Joseph Catalano, *A Commentary of Jean-Paul Sartre's Being and Nothingness* (Chicago: Chicago and London UP, 1974) 7-8.

[4] H. Gene Blocker, *Metaphysics of Absurdity* (Washington D. C.: America UP, 1979) 68.

[5] Jean-Paul Sartre, *Being and Nothingness*, trans. Hazel Barnes (New York: Philosophical Library, 1956) 88-89.

[6] Albert Camus, *The Myth of Sisyphus and Other Essays*, trans. Justin O'Brien (New York: Alfred Knopf, 1975) 14.

[7] Jean-Paul Sartre, *What Is Literature?*, trans. Bernard Frechtman (New York: Philosophical Library, 1949) 23-24.

[8] Hazel Barnes, *Humanistic Existentialism* (Lincoln: Nebraska UP, 1956) 11-13.

[9] Jean-Paul Sartre, *Nausea*, trans. Lloyd Alexander (New York: New Directions Publishing Corp., 1964) 10-11. In further references to this work in CHAPTER III, I will use page numbers only

[10] Colin Wilson, *The Outsider* (Boston: Houghton Mifflin Co., 1956) 25.

[11] Hazel Barnes, *An Existentialist Ethics* (New York: Alfred A. Knopf, 1967) 445.

[12] Philip Thody, *Jean-Paul Sartre: A Literary and Political Study* (London: Hamish Hamilton, 1972) 6.

[13] Hazel Barnes, *Sartre* (New York: J. B. Lippincott Co., 1973) 39.

[14] See, for example, Alfred Stern, *Sartre: His Philosophy and Existential Psychoanalysis* (New York: Dell Publishing Co., 1967) 30-37; Barnes, *Humanistic Existentialism* 197; Blocker 82-88.

NOTES

[15] Wylie Sypher, *Comedy: The Meanings of Comedy* (New York: Doubleday Anchor Books, 1956) 196.

[16] Max Eastman, *Sense of Humor* (New York: Charles Scribner's Sons, 1921) 61.

[17] Jean-Paul Sartre, *The Family Idiot*, trans. Carol Cosman, 4 vols. (Chicago and London: U of Chicago P, 1981-1991) 3: 205.

[18] Philip Thody, *Sartre: A Biographical Introduction* (New York: Charles Scribner's Sons, 1971) 46.

CHAPTER IV

THE STRANGER; THE MYTH OF SISYPHUS

Of all the existentialist writers I am concerned with in my discussion, Albert Camus is perhaps the most controversial. After World War II, Camus was classified as an existentialist; but he disclaimed any such label in an interview he gave to Jeanine Delpech, part of which appeared in *Les Nouvelles Littéraires* in 1945.[1] However, such critics as Hazel Barnes, John Cruickshank, and Philip Thody disagree. Barnes states:

> Henri Peyre evidently shares my belief that one may profitably read Camus in the light of existentialism. His summing up of the problem is formulated in two brief statements with which I am in full agreement. "Albert Camus refused repeatedly to be labeled an existentialist. But for all practical purposes he is one, at least in his philosophy of the absurd, in his constructive and moral pessimism, in his portrayal of the alienated man in *L'Etranger* (*The Stranger*), and in his plays." Some pages later, "We have already noted that Camus never belonged to the existentialist 'sect' and did not subscribe to the (undefined) creed of the group. But, in fact, he matured in the same ideological climate, hailed the same masters (Nietzsche, Kafka, Kierkegaard, and Husserl), shared the same general assumptions: the death of God, unconcern for essence and stress upon existence, the absurd, humanism in the sense that the man freed from belief in God must love and serve all men all the better, and so forth.[2]

54

Cruickshank concurs:

> There was, in fact, a good deal of similarity between the broad
> philosophical tendencies of Camus and Sartre. Both maintained
> an atheistic and humanist position, rejecting moral and meta-
> physical absolutes. They found their value in experience, not in
> *a priori* reasoning, and they had confidence in man's ability to
> fulfill himself without supernatural aid.[3]

In view of the rejection of the supernatural element, Philip Thody also comments about Camus:

> In saying that it [*The Myth of Sisyphus*] "was directed against
> existentialist thinkers" Camus was drawing our attention to the
> fact that its main purpose was to condemn the way in which
> these thinkers introduced hope and transcendence—particularly
> the Christian hope of eternal life—into a world in which there
> were no answers and death was final.[4]

From these various critics, we understand that Camus's intent not to be
classified as an existentialist in fact clashes with the defined reality of existentialism, and, therefore, places him in the absurd position of being an existentialist. Or one could say that Camus's "feeling" of not being an existentialist is contrasted to the general "notion" that he is an existentialist.
Paradoxically, from this confrontation or disparity between "feeling" and
"notion," there arises the experience of the absurd in Camus's own life and
work; it is in such a perspective that I should like to discuss *The Stranger*
and *The Myth of Sisyphus*.

Camus, like all of the existentialist writers I have discussed thus far, experimented with different literary genres in order to explain and describe his
ideas on the absurd. But Camus especially found popularity as a novelist,
and it is in this context that he is known to the general public.[5] Yet Camus's
success as a novelist when he published *The Stranger* is quite ironic. The oc-
cupation of France by Germany during World War II and this novel's lack-
luster themes, expounding a lack of hope, a meaningless world, and a denial
of God, seemed to fit the times; but his creation of a "stranger" on the
fringes of society who refuses to lie, who contents himself with swimming in
the sea, and who expresses an overt optimism were obviously overlooked. In
fact Sartre, Camus's contemporary and sometimes quarrelsome rival in post-
war France, began to express some of these themes and commented upon the

popularity of Camus's abilities as a novelist in a critical essay praising *The Stranger*:

> There is not a single unnecessary detail, not one that is not re-
> turned to later on and used in the argument. And when we close
> the book, we realize that it could not have had any other ending.
> In this world that has been stripped of its causality and pre-
> sented as absurd, the smallest incident has weight. There is no
> single one which does not help to lead its hero to crime and
> capital punishment. *The Stranger* is a classical work, an orderly
> work, composed about the absurd and against the absurd.[6]

To describe fully *The Stranger*, a novel published in 1942, Camus also wrote *The Myth of Sisyphus* as a companion piece, the novel to express in subjective human terms what the essay was to explain in rational and philo-sophical terms. In other words, the novel described the "feeling" of the absurd, whereas the essay explained the "notion" of the absurd. Camus explains:

> The feeling of the absurd is not, for all that, the notion of the
> absurd. It lays the foundation for it, and that is all. It is not lim-
> ited to that notion, except in the brief moment when it passes
> judgment on the universe. Subsequently it has a chance of going
> further. It is alive; in other words, it must die or reverberate.[7]

Sartre's comments on the above passage are also noteworthy:

> *The Stranger* is not an explanatory book. The absurd man does
> not explain; he describes. Nor is it a book which proves any-
> thing.
>   Camus is simply presenting something and is not concerned
> with a justification of what is fundamentally unjustifiable. *The
> Myth of Sisyphus* teaches us how to accept our author's novel.
> In it, we find the theory of the novel of absurdity. Although the
> absurdity of the human condition is its sole theme, it is not a
> novel with a message; it does not come out of a "satisfied" kind
> of thinking, intent on furnishing formal proofs. It is rather the
> product of a thinking which is "limited, rebellious, and mortal."
> It is proof in itself of the futility of abstract reason. (111)

Camus certainly expounds these ideas when he further states in his essay:

> But in fact the preference they [novelists] have shown for writ-
> ing in images rather than in reasoned arguments is revelatory of
> a certain thought that is common to them all, convinced of the
> uselessness of any principle of explanation and sure of the ed-
> ucative message of perceptible appearance. (*Myth* 101)

Since the novel was published before the essay, we can conclude that the
"feeling" of the absurd immerses us in the "climate" of the absurd; hence the
essay follows and illuminates the "landscape."

Given the above, my concern is to explore the extent of the foundation
that the essay develops in terms of the novel, and to see how the novel goes
beyond this foundation even to the point of briefly passing "judgment on the
universe." In other words, in the preface to *The Myth of Sisyphus*, Camus
claims to be a moralist rather than a philosopher: a moralist in the sense of
not dealing with absolutes, but in the sense of describing one person's approach to life. In a critique of *Nausea*, Camus reinforces this moralist position when he says:

> A novel is never anything but a philosophy expressed in im-
> ages. And in a good novel the philosophy has disappeared into
> the images. [...] Nonetheless, a work that is to endure cannot do
> without profound ideas. And this secret fusion of experience
> and thought, of life and reflection on the meaning of life, is
> what makes the great novelists.[8]

If the above is true, is there some sort of harmony between feelings and
ideas, between artistic creation and philosophy which overlap and point towards morality in one's confrontation with the absurd? This is where we
must finally push our investigation.

The most definitive statements Camus makes about confronting the absurd and not committing suicide are found in the beginning of *The Myth of
Sisyphus*: "The absurd depends as much on man as on the world." A few
pages later Camus goes on to say: "The absurd is born of this confrontation
between the human need and the unreasonable silence of the world." From
these statements we can once again deduce that there is a rift between
thought and reality, which springs from the experience of the feeling of the
absurd. Camus is demonstrating the inadequacy of reason to define human
existence: "Between the certainty I have of my existence and the content I

try to give to that assurance, the gap will never be filled. Forever I shall be a stranger to myself" (*Myth* 19). Elsewhere in this essay Camus also states:

> What, then, is that incalculable feeling that deprives the mind of sleep necessary to life? A world that can be explained even with bad reasons is a familiar world. But, on the other hand, in a universe suddenly divested of illusions and lights, man feels an alien, a stranger. (6)

The use of the word "stranger" in the above two passages is important because this divorce between the "head" and the "heart" (using Unamuno's terminology) and between thought and reality characterizes the life and personality of Meursault, the protagonist in *The Stranger*.

Briefly stated, *The Stranger* is divided into two halves. The first half recounts the routine life of Meursault, an office clerk who lives in Algiers. At the outset of the novel, he receives a telegram announcing his mother's death at an old people's home in Marengo about eighty kilometers from Algiers. He obtains a two-day leave of absence from work, attends the wake and funeral, and returns home. After his return home, Meursault goes to a public pool, meets a girl, Marie (a former secretary in his office), and starts an amorous relationship with her. He also gets involved with the affairs of a pimp, Raymond Sintès, a neighbor in his apartment building. One day Meursault, Marie, and Raymond go to visit some of Raymond's friends at the beach. While there, Meursault shoots and kills a knife-wielding Arab, the brother of an Algerian Arab girl Raymond had been mistreating. The second half of the book depicts Meursault's confinement in prison, his trial, including the various witnesses who testify for and against Meursault, and the pronouncement of the death sentence by guillotine for his supposed criminal acts. The last few pages of the novel recount Meursault's revelation concerning life and death.

In a preface written for the 1956 American University edition of *The Stranger*, Camus says:

> I summarized *The Stranger* a long time ago, with a remark that I admit was highly paradoxical: "In our society any man who does not weep at his mother's funeral runs the risk of being sentenced to death." I only meant that the hero of my book is condemned because he does not play the game. In this respect, he is foreign to the society in which he lives; he wanders, on the fringes, in the suburbs of private, solitary, sensual life. (*Lyrical*

335-36)

If the above is true, then my concern in harmonizing Camus's novel and essay in respect to the absurd must center on this passage and the ideas and feelings it evokes.

In *The Myth of Sisyphus*, Camus describes various experiences of the absurd:

> In certain situations, replying "nothing" when asked what one is thinking about may be a pretense in man. [...] But if that reply is sincere, if it symbolizes that odd state of soul in which the void becomes eloquent, in which the chain of daily gestures is broken, in which the heart vainly seeks the link that will connect it again, then it is as it were the first sign of absurdity. (12)

From Camus's first notion of the absurd, there are many parallels to *The Stranger*, concerning Meursault's feeling of the absurd while at his mother's funeral. For example, before the wake, Meursault is asked once by the warden of the home and another time by the doorkeeper if he would like to see his mother's body, but either he doesn't respond or he replies in the negative. Upon being questioned by the doorkeeper, Meursault responds, "Well, really I couldn't say."[9] The critic Colin Wilson says Meursault lacks feeling, and this lack is manifest in Meursault's indifference to life.[10] Yet Wilson misses something here. It is better to say that Meursault shuns introspection, because he honestly trusts in the reality of his senses. If there is any lack in Meursault's life, it is the lack of unity and conformity. Such a lack is indicative of the absurd.

Meursault is simply uncertain about things, and he relies on the spontaneity of life to define his actions. In other words, by portraying Meursault as an authentically direct person with few analytical powers, Camus gives us a strong impression of the "void" felt by someone who experiences the absurd. In fact, Meursault does make the comment later in the story that "of recent years, I'd rather lost the habit of noting my feelings, and hardly knew what to say" (80). Also, if critics say that Meursault is indifferent to his mother's death, showing no grief, it is only because they too are applying their value judgments of sentimentality to his actions. Hazel Barnes says:

> Camus is not arguing that it is desirable for human beings to be so close to indifference, but that in a world where this is the truth about most human relationships, Meursault is, in Socratic

fashion, ahead of those who pretend that things are other than they are. (179)

Meursault refuses to say anything more than what is personally true for him. Instead he focuses on his sensual experiences during the wake and funeral: the uncomfortable glare of the lights off the white walls in the mortuary, his desire to drink café au lait and smoke cigarettes during the wake, and the uncomfortable heat of the sun reflecting off of the road he must walk along in route to his mother's interment. Meursault's silence is also the result of a natural, personal, human experience because he is tired from the journey: he falls asleep on the bus ride to the home and at the wake.

A final observation regarding Meursault's silence comes from a statement about his relationship with his mother: "When we lived together, Mother was always watching me, but we hardly ever talked" (3-4). According to Sartre in *Being and Nothingness*, the "look" of the "Other" indicates she has been turning Meursault into an object, by stealing his world from him, that is the world he accepts as his own because he is a subject, a center of the world. Her silence in life and now in death also demonstrates that Meursault is now free from the condemning gaze of the "Other." In this instance her look, turning Meursault into an object, is now ironically echoed in Meursault's refusal to look at her corpse. Yet this can be viewed in a positive way because later in the story, at the trial, Meursault does state that he liked his mother and is sorry she is now dead. These statements do indicate his refusal to sit in moral judgment upon their past relationship which, according to Meursault, could very well have been one of amiability on his part. This is also implied at the trial when he says that he sent her to the old people's home because he didn't have sufficient funds to make sure that she was suitably cared for at their apartment.

The idea of the "look" is also reinforced when the inmates of the home attend the wake:

> [T]hey looked at me, and wagged their heads awkwardly [...]. I inclined to think that they were greeting me, after their fashion, but it had a queer effect, seeing all those old fellows grouped round the keeper, solemnly eyeing me and dandling their heads from side to side. For a moment I had an absurd impression that they had come to sit in judgment on me. (11)

Once again in the chapter "The Look" in *Being and Nothingness*, Sartre explains an experience which is strikingly similar to this. Sartre defines

Meursault's position as a stranger in society who refuses to conceptualize his feelings:

> Let us each one refer to his own experience. There is no one who has not at some time been surprised in an attitude which was guilty or simply ridiculous. The abrupt modification then experienced was in no way provoked by the irruption of knowledge. It is rather in itself a solidification and an abrupt stratification of myself which leaves intact my possibilities and my structures "for-myself," but which suddenly pushes me into a new dimension of existence—the dimension of the *unrevealed.* [...] This term, [...] of a free Other, is itself an infinite and inexhaustible synthesis of unrevealed properties. Through the Other's look I *live* myself as fixed in the midst of the world, as in danger, as irremediable. But I *know* neither what I am nor what is my place in the world, nor what face this world in which I am turns toward the Other.[11]

As the inmates' judgment of Meursault implies the negative, turning their heads from side to side as they look at him, Meursault's denial of any judgment, his nodding off to sleep, implies an affirmation in life in which the "void becomes eloquent." The twofold "no" of the inmates and "yes" of Meursault combine to show the constant disparity of life—the absurd—in terms of thought and judgment (the inmates) and feeling and awareness (Meursault).

A further consideration in *The Myth of Sisyphus* and another notion of the absurd concerns mechanical living. Camus states:

> Rising, streetcar, four hours in the office or the factory, meal, streetcar, four hours of work, meal, sleep, and Monday Tuesday Wednesday Thursday Friday and Saturday according to the same rhythm [...]. But one day the "why" arises and everything begins in that weariness tinged with amazement. [...] Weariness comes at the end of a mechanical life, but at the same time it inaugurates the impulse of consciousness. (*Myth* 12-13)

In *The Stranger*, since Meursault is an office worker, usually eats his meals at Celeste's restaurant, and takes the streetcar to work, the parallels to Camus's essay are obvious. What is not so obvious is how Meursault breaks out of the chain of events and realizes his absurd consciousness. At the beginning of Chapter II Meursault realizes why his employer appeared angry when he asked for two days off to attend the funeral. This means that Meursault gets four days off from work, since the wake is on a Thursday and the funeral is on a Friday. It is readily apparent that Meursault has broken out of the chain of daily events because of his mother's death. Especially noteworthy is the Sunday Meursault spends roaming around his apartment at "loose ends" after his return home. This is the "anxiety" Camus speaks of in reference to Heidegger and the absurd. Since the absurd is the product of Meursault's consciousness confronting reality (his mother's death), his awareness of the world after her death is important.

As Meursault roams about his apartment, one of the central things he does is to observe the people down on the street below. The view from his bedroom looks out upon the central street in the neighborhood. Previously it had been raining, but the weather changes and everything now glistens in the afternoon sun. The people he observes below seem to be in an absurd rush as they scurry around town. Here we see Meursault's awareness of people living mechanically juxtaposed to him doing nothing except observing. As people go to the matinees for a film, the stadium for a soccer match, or just for a walk, Meursault notes that this is a "typical Sunday afternoon" for them. As a corollary to this position, later in the story, Meursault encounters the "robot woman" while he is dining at Celeste's restaurant. Described as a peculiar-looking woman, she enters the establishment, walking as if she were somehow connected to wires, and asks to sit at Meursault's table; he complies. She orders food, pays for it in advance, and eats ravenously, checking off certain programs from a radio magazine, oblivious to Meursault's scrutiny of her. She leaves, and Meursault, highly intrigued by her oddity, follows her for a while down the street until he can no longer keep up with her brisk, mechanical movements.

In contrast to these mechanical aspects of living, it is important to note Meursault's awareness of other people's routine actions: his consciousness indicates that "awareness is what matters; there is no ultimately deeper satisfaction than man's conscious and deliberate consent to the full intensity of experience, no matter what its quality" (Barnes 170). In another essay entitled "The Wrong Side and the Right Side," Camus explains: "What I wish for now is no longer happiness but simply awareness" (*Lyrical* 61). To most people, the loss of a mother produces emotional outbursts, accompanied with profound introspection about their former past experiences together. For Meursault something unique transpires: his life is not struck with the absurd by an introspective look into his past, but it is experienced moment by moment. Each successive feeling goes hand in hand with each successive moment; he lives a discontinuous succession of present moments. Camus explains this idea in *The Myth of Sisyphus*: "The present and succession of presents before a constantly conscious soul is the ideal of the absurd man" (63-64). This philosophical notion is portrayed in purely human terms for the reader from Meursault's last impressions at the end of the second chapter: "It occurred to me that somehow I'd got through another Sunday, that Mother now was buried, and tomorrow I'd be going back to work as usual. Really, nothing in my life had changed" (30).

· The next notion of the absurd Camus speaks of in his essay concerns the passage of time:

> Yet a day comes when a man notices or says that he is thirty.
> Thus he asserts his youth. But simultaneously he situates himself in relation to time. He takes his place in it. [...] He belongs to time, and by the horror that seizes him, he recognizes his worst enemy. (*Myth* 13-14)

Given the above, we do find out that Meursault is thirty years old, and we know he has a tedious job doing bills of lading as a clerk in an office. In what seems a direct address to the novel, Camus says in *The Myth of Sisyphus* (68) that "a subclerk in the post office is the equal of a conqueror if consciousness is common to them." This idea becomes critically important in the second half of the novel, while Meursault is in prison: he does not lose track of time, unlike other prisoners. It is at this point that a shift occurs in Meursault's life. Since he is deprived of his freedom and has a lot of spare time on his hands, Meursault finally becomes more introspective. Meursault reflects:

> Yet again, the whole problem was: how to kill time. After a while, however, once I'd learn the trick of remembering things, I never had a moment's boredom. [...]
> So I learned that even after a single day's experience of the outside world a man could easily live a hundred years in prison. He'd have laid up enough memories never to be bored. (98-99)

From this passage, Camus is affirming that human life, reduced to a measurable span of time, is an elementary value in the world that has personal importance. The finite length of Meursault's life while in prison gives him conscious awareness of the only true value he can know with any positive certainty, his own life. Micheline Tisson-Braun explains: "Thus not consciousness but personal consciousness would bring about the rift and the discrepancy that are felt as absurdity."[12] This is part of the reason Meursault doesn't know his mother's age because the time that one lives (on a personal level) cannot be experienced vicariously. The opening of the story, including the telegram that Meursault receives, reinforces this idea:

> Mother died today. Or, maybe, yesterday; I can't be sure. The telegram from the Home says: YOUR MOTHER PASSED AWAY. FUNERAL TOMORROW. DEEP SYMPATHY. Which leaves the matter doubtful; it could have been yesterday. (1)

Both of the above examples point to society's attempt "to create a continuous time and a logical world."[13] This becomes concrete for the reader as Meursault reflects about some of his mother's maxims as he whiles away the time in jail: "In the long run one gets used to anything" (96), and "however miserable one is, there's always something to be thankful for" (142). It is from these perspectives that Meursault finds value in his life and confronts the passage of time. In other words, he seeks to "kill time" in order to live more. Also, while in prison, a remark summarizes Meursault's awareness that time is an unmitigated evil: "And something I'd been told came back; a remark made by the nurse at Mother's funeral. No there was no way out, and no one can imagine what the evenings are like in prison" (101). It is logical to assume that Meursault's contentment in living passively is mixed with the dread of time passing by, and each feeling is contributing to the other.

Camus, like Sartre, felt that nature can negate us, thereby creating consciousness of the absurd upon our perception of this phenomenon.[14] Camus explains in his essay:

> At the heart of all beauty lies something inhuman, and these hills, the softness of the sky, the outline of these trees at this very minute lose the illusory meaning with which we had clothed them, henceforth more remote than a lost paradise. [...] The world evades us because it becomes itself again. That stage scenery masked by habit becomes again what it is. It withdraws at a distance from us. (*Myth* 14)

Returning to my central image again, the sun on the day of the funeral is fiery hot and the air is heating up quickly. Presently, Meursault begins to notice that as the sun beats down on the surrounding landscape, the area

takes on an eerie and foreboding appearance. This central image of the unbearable, hot Algerian sun will be repeated in the story: the day Meursault
shoots the Arab on the beach, and during the three days of Meursault's trial.
I will examine these three instances in detail to show, through a confrontation with the absurd in nature, Meursault's attempt to flee must end in failure
because the absurd fades away when he ceases to acknowledge it.

In the beginning of *The Stranger*, the bright lamps that are brought in for
the wake foreshadow Meursault's confrontation with the sun at the funeral
proceedings. When the keeper switches on the lamps, Meursault is blinded
by the intense light. Later, Meursault asks if some of the lamps could be
turned off because the reflection off of the light-colored walls hurts his eyes.
In response, the keeper refuses and comments that he prefers to leave them
all on or off, no compromising the situation. Walking to the cemetery the
next day, Meursault has intense discomfort again as the blazing sun takes up
the role played by the bright lamps. The sun becomes an antagonist to
Meursault, symbolizing not only discomfort but alienation. Once again the
nurse's words to Meursault prove prophetic because if he walks too slow, he
is susceptible to sunstroke; but if he goes too fast, he sweats, and later the
brisk air in the church will make him cold: one way or another nature will
take its toll. Subsequently, experiencing the absurd in nature is threatening
for Meursault, and he seeks respite from the sun. At the conclusion of the funeral, Meursault immediately boards the bus home, failing to linger at the
grave as the others leave. In route to Algiers, we learn of his simple satisfaction as he enters the city at night, lit up by the street lamps. Meursault has
momentarily escaped the sun's onslaught and its alienating power, seeking
relief and comfort in his home town during the cool of the evening.

In contrast to the above, we can point out that Meursault does enjoy the
sun, but only when he is by the sea. This is important if we look at the in-
terplay of the French words for sun—*le soleil*—and sea—*la mer*.[15] The sun,
a masculine image, is something he seeks to escape from by immersing himself in the sea, a feminine image. Anytime Meursault and Marie go to the
beach, he is very content to be in the water: to cool off, so to speak, because
of the heat of the discomforting and alienating sun. Thus, Meursault's name
in French evokes homophonically "only sea" or *mer seule*. Furthermore, the
word "sea"—*la mer*—is a homonym for the word "mother"—*la mère*.
Therefore, returning to my former discussion of a lack in Meursault's life, it
is logical to say that Meursault is seeking that which he now lacks, a mother;
and he is fleeing from that which he has too much of, the sun or alienation.
This will be more obvious in Meursault's next major confrontation with the
sun: the killing of the Arab.

As Chapter VI begins, Meursault and Marie are preparing to go to the beach with Raymond in order to visit some of Raymond's friends, the Massons, who have a cabin at the seaside. From the outset of their journey, Marie tells Meursault that he looks like "a mourner at a funeral." At the beach, while Meursault, Raymond, and Masson stroll along the sand, there is an altercation with an Arab, the brother of Raymond's Algerian mistress, and Raymond is cut with a knife by the Arab. Afterwards Meursault decides to go for a walk along the beach alone, carrying Raymond's revolver, and he encounters this same Arab. The description of the heat from the sun as the two men meet on the beach is crucial because, scorching down on Meursault, the sun causes him to perspire again and sweat forms on his face, and this duplicates the heat he has formerly experienced at this mother's funeral. The link is now made to the funeral, and we know Meursault wants to flee from this encounter with the sun because it is alienating, uncomfortable, and blinding. The Arab pulls out his knife again, and the reflection of the sunlight off of the knife sends Meursault into a frenzy:

> I was conscious only of the cymbals of the sun clashing on my skull, and, less distinctly, of the keen blade of light flashing up from the knife, scarring my eyelashes, and gouging into my eyeballs. [...] Every nerve in my body was a steel spring, and my grip closed on the revolver. The trigger gave, and the smooth underbelly of the butt jogged my palm. And so, with that crisp, whipcrack sound, it all began. I shook off my sweat and the clinging veil of light. I knew I'd shattered the balance of the day [...]. (75-76)

The last few sentences of this passage are important because we wonder after the shot why "it all began," and how he has shattered the "balance of the day." These two phrases go hand in hand. If the sun is the primary cause of the murder—a sign of the absurd—then Meursault has upset the balance of the day by adhering to a different set of norms than those established by the society in which he lives.[16] In other words, Meursault kills the Arab without reason and moves toward the counterbalancing force of personal feeling which society dislikes. The phrase "it all began" suggests that society will not tolerate Meursault's actions and feelings because he does not "play the game" according to their rules. He must conform or society will dispose of him; the farcical trial Meursault must undergo for society will accomplish this.

The first day of the trial is filled with sunshine, and the hot air is unbearable, much like on the day of his mother's funeral and when Meursault shot the Arab. In spite of the heat, Meursault does notice the jury, and he perceives that they are staring at him, possibly viewing him as a criminal.

From this description, another one of Camus's notions of the absurd emerges. This concerns the strangeness of other people negating us by their actions. Camus explains in *The Myth of Sisyphus*:

> Men, too, secrete the inhuman. At certain moments of lucidity, the mechanical aspect of their gestures, their meaningless pantomime makes silly everything that surrounds them. [...] This incalculable tumble before the image of what we are, this "nausea, as a writer of today calls it, is also the absurd. (14-15)

As I stated in chapter three, the link to Sartre's *Nausea* is evident from the above remarks, as is the experience of being contingent (*de trop*) while in the midst of other people. In words Sartre might well have used, Camus depicts Meursault looking around the courtroom and reflecting:

> Just then I noticed that almost all the people in the courtroom were greeting each other, exchanging remarks and forming groups—behaving, in fact, as in a club where the company of others of one's own tastes and standing makes one feel at ease. That, no doubt, explained the odd impression I had of being *de trop* here, a sort of gate-crasher. (104-05)

It is the people in the world (as well as the objects in the world) which negate Meursault, culminating in a guilty verdict as the trial proceeds for the next few days.

We know, of course, that Meursault is not tried for the murder of the Arab. Instead he is tried, convicted and sentenced to death for not weeping at his mother's funeral, not knowing her age, and smoking cigarettes and drinking café au lait at the wake. Furthermore, the prosecution attempts to prove that the murder was premeditated since the accused started a romantic liaison with Marie the day after the funeral and he consorted with a pimp. During the three days of the trial, the heat continues to be unbearable and stifling for Meursault, causing much discomfort and alienation. At one point in the proceedings, the judge finally asks Meursault why he shot the Arab. Meursault's response, "because of the sun," provokes laughter in the courtroom, yet Meursault finds nothing comical about this remark and remains stolid. In his book *On Aggression*, the natural scientist Konrad Lorenz discusses laughter in a situation strikingly parallel to that of Meursault at the trial:

> Laughter produces, simultaneously, a strong fellow feeling among participants and joint aggressiveness against outsiders. Heartily laughing together at the same thing forms an immediate bond, much as enthusiasm for the same ideal does. Finding the same thing funny is not only a prerequisite to a real friendship, but very often the first step to its formation. Laughter forms a bond and simultaneously draws a line. If you cannot laugh with others, you feel an outsider [...]. If laughter is in fact directed at an outsider, as in scornful derision, the component of aggressive motivation and, at the same time, the analogy to certain forms of the triumph ceremony become greatly enhanced.[17]

The word "outsider" that Lorenz uses in his discussion of the alienating qualities of laughter is most pertinent here, considering that some translations of *L'Etranger* in English use the title *The Outsider* instead of *The Stranger*.[18] Also important in Lorenz's discussion are two important details which have direct relevance to Meursault's trial: the laughter is a social gesture—a form of rational self-defense—against Meursault's absurd experience in reference to the sun because the onlookers are threatened by Meursault's nonconformity to their social norms. Sartre concurs on this point in *The Family Idiot*: "But laughter is a collective reaction [...] by which a group threatened with some danger withdraws solidarity from the man in whom the danger is incarnate."[19] Secondly, their laughter (since it is meant to be a corrective) makes Meursault realize that these people loathe him because he revolts against the serious world which they represent, since he asserts his freedom. The jury especially does not comprehend that Meursault's love of life is more important than an aggressive show of laughter. In reference again to Camus's essay on the absurd and how people "secrete the inhuman," accompanied by the feeling of "nausea." Meursault, desolate at this point, gets so caught up in the trial that he feels like vomiting. Now, he merely wants to get the entire ordeal over with and go back to his prison cell.

The significance of Meursault's flight from the sun (at his mother's funeral, while shooting the Arab on the beach, and during the three days of unbearable heat at his trial) is ultimately related to the notion of death. Camus explains death and the absurd in *The Myth of Sisyphus*:

I come at last to death and to the attitude we have toward it. [...]
This is because in reality there is no experience of death.
Properly speaking, nothing has been experienced but what has
been lived and made conscious. [...] From this inert body on
which a slap makes no mark the soul has disappeared. This elementary and definitive aspect of the adventure constitutes the
absurd feeling. Under the fatal lighting of that destiny, its use-
lessness becomes evident. (15-16)

The last sentence of the above passage with the key words "fatal lighting" are symbolic of the sun in *The Stranger*. If the sun represents light,
lucidity, or knowledge, we know Meursault's former attempts to flee from
this knowledge of death have been futile. He must live the experience of the
sun by opening himself to this knowledge, a natural source for him to dwell
in. It is not until the death sentence has been passed that he finally confronts
the knowledge of his death and faces the absurd. Philip Thody explains:

For Meursault the absurd is essentially the result of his awareness of his own mortality, of what Camus calls, in *Le Mythe de
Sisyphe,* the "bloodstained mathematics which dominate the
human lot." He is the "everyday man" described in the essay
who, before his discovery of the absurd, had projects, hopes,
ambitions, the belief that he was free to order his life, but who
has realised that "all that is disproved in one breath-taking
sweep by the absurdity of a possible death." (*Albert* 39)

Indeed, Philip Thody is correct if we observe Meursault's reflections after
the trial:

Try as I might, I couldn't stomach this brutal certitude. For really, when one came to think of it, there was a disproportion between the judgment on which it was based and the unalterable
sequence of events starting from the moment when that judgment was delivered. (137)

The cycle is now complete: beginning with his mother's funeral, shooting
the Arab, and the sentencing to death by guillotine, Meursault has been
haunted by death, but never able to experience it firsthand through rational
knowledge. This helps explain why Meursault refused to see his mother's
body: he cannot truly experience death through viewing her corpse. Finally,

while waiting for his execution, Meursault preoccupies himself with thoughts about "circumventing the machine." Serge Doubrovsky (155) explains: "Threatened with annihilation, life gathers and concentrates its force, becomes conscious of itself and proclaims that it is the only value." It is also interesting to note that Meursault's only reflections about his father, whom Meursault never knew, surface at this time. Meursault remembers a story that his mother told him once about his father's attendance at an execution: his father later came home and was violently sick. Now Meursault concludes if he ever gets out of jail (through a loophole), he will go to every execution that takes place. In other words, the horror of his impending death resides in Meursault's desire to live because he finally harmonizes his thoughts and feelings, thus confronting the absurd.

Concerning the three consequences of the absurd in *The Myth of Sisyphus*—revolt, freedom, and passion—they can be best summarized in the novel in the final scene, with the confrontation between Meursault and the prison chaplain. Briefly stated, Meursault has refused to see the chaplain three times, and the chaplain finally comes to Meursault's cell unannounced. The chaplain asks why Meursault has refused any religious help, and Meursault replies that he doesn't believe in God. The chaplain then wants to know how Meursault will face death, and the prisoner responds that he will confront it precisely as he is doing so now at this point in his life. He is startled by Meursault's lack of hope and asks if after one dies, there is nothing remaining: Meursault responds affirmatively. The chaplain feels that Meursault is now burdened with guilt and must rid himself of this feeling. He wants to know if Meursault has seen a divine face on the wall of the cell, and Meursault says that he has only seen the face of Marie on the wall. He speaks of an afterlife and wants to know if Meursault has wished for this. Meursault agrees, but adds that this wish has no more importance than a person wanting to be wealthy, to be a fast swimmer, or to have a shapely mouth. Finally, the chaplain wants to know what kind of afterlife Meursault might conjure up in his mind, and Meursault shouts back that he would like to have a life similar to the one he has known here on this earth. Meursault turns violent and starts shouting with a mixture of glee and anger about people who seem to be so certain of themselves about life after death, and says that none of the chaplain's certainties is worth anything substantial. Meursault divulges all of his past thoughts, thinking that the chaplain lived like a zombie and couldn't be certain of his existence. In contrast, Meursault is sure of his own existence, yet understands his contingency and the certainty of his own death that is sure to come. Meursault rails about the fact that he spent his own life in one way rather than another; and he notes the dim forecast which, like a constant wind, had been coming toward him throughout his life, including the days that are yet to come. Finally, he wants to know what difference it could possibly make if, after being convicted of murder, the state kills him for not crying at his mother's funeral. Hearing all the shouting, the jailers rush into the cell to pull the chaplain away from Meursault's grasp.

Meursault's intense burst of emotion indicates his passionate awakening to "a new awareness of himself and of life" (Barnes 185). From this conscious awareness of the absurd, he revolts against the chaplain's preconceived ideas of life after death, full of false hope and a determined future. Subsequently, Meursault's anger provides a catharsis which cleanses his emotions, strips him of any future hope, and frees him "to cultivate the pure flame of life itself" (Barnes 186).

Afterward, sitting in his cell, Meursault understands his revolt, freedom, and passion in terms of his mother's actions at the end of her life:

> I understood why at her life's end she had taken on a fiancé; why she played at making a fresh start. [...] With death so near, mother must have felt like someone on the brink of freedom, ready to start life all over again. No one, no one in the world had any right to weep for her. And I, too, felt ready to start life all over again. [...] I laid my heart open to the benign indifference of the universe. To feel it so like myself, indeed, so brotherly, made me realize that I'd been happy, and that I was happy still. (153-54)

Meursault, like Sisyphus, opens his heart to the "benign indifference of the universe," and one must imagine both men "happy" because they cease making rational demands upon an irrational world. Instead they revel in their revolt, freedom, and passion, which they give to their individual lives, in order to create personal happiness. In other words, both men possess *disponibilité*. This word occurs quite frequently in existentialist literature and means "availability." Camus explains in *The Myth of Sisyphus*:

> The divine availability of the condemned man before whom the prison doors open in a certain early dawn, that unbelievable disinterestedness with regard to everything except for the pure flame of life—it is clear that death and the absurd are here the principles of the only reasonable freedom: that which a human heart can experience and live. (59-60)

The "divine availability" that Camus speaks of in the above passage can be better explained in relationship to Meursault's revolt, freedom and passion if I return again to the 1956 preface Camus wrote for *The Stranger*. Camus says:

> A much more accurate idea of the character [...] will emerge if one asks just *how* Meursault doesn't play the game. The reply is a simple one: he refuses to lie. To lie is not only to say what isn't true. It is also and above all, to say *more* than is true, and, as far as the human heart is concerned, to express more than one feels. [...] Far from being bereft of all feeling, he is animated by a passion that is deep because it is stubborn, a passion for the absolute and for truth. [...]
>
> One would therefore not be much mistaken to read *The Stranger* as the story of a man who, without any heroics, agrees to die for the truth. I also happened to say, again paradoxically, that I had tried to draw in my character the only Christ we deserve. (*Lyrical* 336-37)

Camus's moralist position that I referred to earlier in this chapter is now explicit. Meursault is an individual who pursues his own personal truth: a passion for a beautiful young woman and swimming in the sea, a freedom to express or not express what he is aware of or feels, and a revolt against any society, steeped in pettiness and abstraction, which condemns him for his individual passion and freedom. Although Camus would deny Kierkegaard's "leap of faith," the latter does say something remarkably similar to Camus's preface:

> The crowd is untruth. Therefore was Christ crucified because although He addressed himself to all, He would have no dealings with the crowd, because He would not permit the crowd to aid him in any way, because in this regard He repelled people absolutely, would not found a party, did not permit balloting, but would be what He is, the Truth, which relates itself to the individual. —And hence every one who truly would serve the truth is *eo ipso*, in one way or another, a martyr. If it were possible for a person in his mother's womb to make a decision to will to serve the truth truly, then, whatever his martyrdom turns out to be, he is *eo ipso* from his mother's womb a martyr. For it is not so great a trick to win the crowd. All that is needed is

some talent, a certain dose of falsehood, and a little acquaintance with human passions. But no witness for the truth.[20]

The moralist position here is so close to that of Camus's preface because Meursault, pure and simple, is presented as a martyr to his own truth.

The most convincing evidence that Camus is a moralist of the absurd in *The Stranger* comes from Sartre:

> He represented in our time the latest example of that long line of *moralistes*. [...] His obstinate humanism, narrow and pure, austere and sensual, waged an uncertain war against the massive and formless events of the time. But on the other hand through his dogged rejections he reaffirmed, at the heart of our epoch, against the Machiavellians and against the Idol of realism the existence of the moral issue. [...]
>
> I call the accident that killed Camus a scandal because it suddenly projects into the center of our human world the absurdity of our most fundamental needs. At the age of twenty, Camus, suddenly afflicted with a malady that upset his whole life, discovered the Absurd—the senseless negation of man. He became accustomed to it, he *thought out* his unbearable condition, he came through. And yet one is tempted to think that only his first works tell the truth about his life, since that invalid once cured is annihilated by an unexpected death from the outside.[21]

Camus's morals in *The Stranger* are not simple guidelines for living but suggest an existential tension between such moralist themes as justice and truth, freedom and happiness, life and death, and availability and non-participation, making the absurd evident in an equilibrium of opposites. This novel and *The Myth of Sisyphus* start to pass one into the other. As affirmation of experience and feeling is made in life (the novel) by not negating the world of reason (the essay), thus balancing the two extremes, Meursault has learned that he cannot sit back and passively exist; he must face this aspect of the absurd, which is not an end but a beginning. The divine face Meursault sees on the wall in his cell is Marie's, a symbol of a relationship and friendship that he would like to continue developing; yet it is not a blending with the crowd. Thinking about his past actions of non-reflexivity, Meursault admits his partial guilt: "For all to be accomplished, for me to feel *less lonely* [my emphasis], all that remained to hope was that on the day of my execution there should be a huge crowd of spectators and that they should greet me with howls of execration" (154).

NOTES

[1] Albert Camus, "Non, je ne suis pas existentialiste," *Les Nouvelles Littéraires* 15 Nov. 1945: 1+.

[2] Hazel Barnes, *Humanistic Existentialism* (Lincoln: Nebraska UP, 1959) 405.

[3] John Cruickshank, *Albert Camus and the Literature of Revolt* (London: Oxford UP, 1960) 120-21.

[4] Philip Thody, *Albert Camus: A Biographical Study* (London: Hamish Hamilton, 1961) 50.

[5] Donald Lazere, *The Unique Creation of Albert Camus* (New Haven and London: Yale UP, 1973) 151-52.

[6] Jean-Paul Sartre, "An Explication of *The Stranger*," *Camus: A Collection of Critical Essays*, ed. Germaine Brée (Englewood Cliffs, N. J.: Prentice-Hall Inc., 1962) 121.

[7] Albert Camus, *The Myth of Sisyphus and Other Essays*, trans. Justin O'Brien (New York: Alfred A. Knopf, 1972) 28.

[8] Albert Camus, *Lyrical and Critical Essays*, trans. Ellen Kennedy, ed. Philip Thody (New York: Alfred A. Knopf, 1968) 199.

[9] Albert Camus, *The Stranger*, trans. Stuart Gilbert (New York: Vintage Books, 1954) 6. In further references to this work in CHAPTER IV, I will use page numbers only.

[10] Colin Wilson, *The Outsider* (Boston: Houghton Mifflin Co., 1956) 28-29.

[11] Jean-Paul Sartre, *Being and Nothingness*, trans. Hazel Barnes (New York: Philosophical Library, 1956) 268.

[12] Micheline Tisson-Braun, "Silence and the Desert: The Flickering Vision," *Critical Essays on Albert Camus*, ed. Robert Lecker (Boston: G. K. Hall & Co., 1988) 44.

[13] Serge Doubrovsky, "The Ethics of Albert Camus," *Critical Essays on Albert Camus*, ed. Robert Lecker (Boston: G. K. Hall & Co., 1988) 155.

[14] The question arises here as to how one should interpret Camus's sense of nature negating humans: because we question and expect an answer

NOTES

from nature and obviously don't get one, this is what negation means. Thus the absurd is the incommensurability of nature and humans.

[15] David Ellison, *Understanding Albert Camus* (Columbia, South Carolina: South Carolina UP, 1990) 63.

[16] Patrick McCarthy, *Albert Camus: The Stranger* (Cambridge: Cambridge UP, 1988) 46.

[17] Konrad Lorenz, *On Aggression* (New York: Harcourt, Brace, and World, 1963) 293-94.

[18] See, for example, Stuart Gilbert's translation of *The Outsider*, in *The Collected Fiction of Albert Camus* (London: Hamish Hamilton, 1960); Philip Thody's commentary is also entitled "The Outsider" in *Albert Camus: A Biographical Study* (London: Hamish Hamilton, 1961).

[19] Jean-Paul Sartre, *The Family Idiot*, trans. Carol Cosman, 4 vols. (Chicago and London: U of Chicago P, 1987) 2:29.

[20] Sören Kierkegaard, "That Individual," *Existentialism from Dostoevsky to Sartre*, ed. Walter Kaufmann (New York: New American Library, 1975) 96-97.

[21] Jean-Paul Sartre, "Tribute to Albert Camus," *Camus: A Collection of Critical Essays*, ed. Germaine Brée (Englewood Cliffs, N. J.: Prentice-Hall, Inc., 1962) 173-74.

CHAPTER V

NATIVE SON

From humble beginnings as a Negro in the South, Richard Wright tried to establish a foothold in the modern world by changing the way Americans viewed minorities. This became manifest through his writing, which reflected what it means to be a human, a refusal of subordination to any racial group in America, and a desire for self-realization. Consequently, his literature brought him into conflict with both the black and white populace, and the various racial barriers each group tried to encircle him with were unsuccessful. Frustrated and scorned, he emigrated to France after World War II and became formally associated with the French existentialist writers. The oppressive racial climate in Europe before the war was similar to that of the continuing ethnic problems in the United States under a dominant, oppressive, and racist white society. Donald Gibson explains:

> In order to understand the sources of the existentialist concern in Wright's work and thought, one need only note the quality and character of the life described by Wright [...] and realize as well that "existentialism" may be described as a mood arising out of the exigencies of certain life situations rather than as a fully developed and articulated systematic philosophy which one chooses to hold or rejects. Though we cannot say that existentialism resulted directly from the experience of Europeans under Nazi occupation, we can certainly say that the occupation, the war itself, created circumstances conducive to the

nurturing and development of the existential response.[1]

Richard Macksey and Frank Moorer concur:

> Wright was, of course, delighted to find in Paris an "engaged"
> intellectual movement that, like his own life, had been so
> clearly forged in the experience of oppression—the movement
> of German prison camps, the Nazi occupation, and the
> Resistance.[2]

The racial conflict Wright experienced is one expression of the absurd
and coincides with the existentialist movement in France. It is the discrepancy between one's ideals and the world's meaningless reality: this is a way
in which one experiences the absurd. The resulting alienation and lack of
meaning is what the French existentialists were describing in their novels
and essays. Likewise, Wright wanted to be at peace with the world (intent),
but he was unable to find the world meaningful because of established social
oppression, keeping him in a constant state of alienation (reality). Like
Meursault in Camus's *The Stranger*, Wright felt himself rootless, a wan-
derer, a stranger to society. As Wright says of himself:

> I'm a rootless man, but I'm neither psychologically distraught
> nor in anywise perturbed because of it [...]. I declare un-
> abashedly that I like and even cherish the state of abandonment,
> of aloneness; it does not bother me; indeed, to me it seems the
> natural, inevitable condition of man. (qtd. in Macksey and
> Moorer 12)

Wright's outlet for this experience of the absurd was his first novel *Native
Son*, published in 1940, two years before Camus's *The Myth of Sisyphus* and
The Stranger.

The question arises as to whether this book is characteristic of existentialist literature, since Wright did not meet Jean-Paul Sartre and Simone de
Beauvoir until after World War II. The critic Robert Bone explains:
"Wright's existentialism is not a foreign graft. Long before he met Sartre or
read Camus he was working in this vein. What occurred in France was the
vindication of his early intuition".[3] Edward Margolies concurs:

> Wright learned as a Negro living in the South that the rules,
> principles, and institutions of white America did not apply to

him. And since he could not accept abject submission as a way of life, he endured a constant state of anxiety, and discovered the necessity of forging for himself his own ethics, his own morality, indeed his own personality, in a world that offered him little security or identity. This has since been called his "existentialism"—French existentialists after World War II seized upon Wright's works to support their own philosophy— but his views were formed long before he knew the meaning of this term.[4]

The above passages, depicting Wright as an existentialist, are certainly credible, but the most authoritative definition of what constitutes an existentialist writer comes from Hazel Barnes. She says that there are three distinctive characteristics that illuminate the literature of humanistic existentialism. First, this literature must work with myth; second, it must concern itself with the basic situations in which human freedom affirms itself; third, it must have a keen sense of social responsibility.[5] If these characteristics hold true, then, *Native Son* must be put to the test in order to see if it merits the existentialist label and inclusion in my study of the absurd.

First, *Native Son* explodes the myth that America is a classless society. Constance Webb, in her biography of Wright, quotes from one of his unpublished speeches: "Perhaps someone will explain how it [is] possible for us to construct the atom bomb and at the same time entertain myths, legends, and downright folk superstitions about race."[6] This myth is based upon one of the primary foundations that "all men are created equal" set forth by Thomas Jefferson when he wrote the Declaration of Independence; however, at the same time this was written America endorsed slavery. Dorothy Fisher makes a similar analysis:

> In other words, our American society creates around all youth (as every society does) a continual pressure of suggestion to try to live up to the accepted ideals of the country—such ordinary, traditional, taken-for-granted American ideals as to fight injustice fearlessly; to cringe to no man; to choose one's own life work; to resist with stouthearted self-respect affronts to decent human dignity, whether one's own or others'; to drive ahead toward honestly earned success, all sails spread to the old American wind blowing from the Declaration of Independence. But our society puts Negro youth in the situation of the animal [...], by making it impossible for him to try to live up to those

never-to-be-questioned national ideals, as other young
Americans do.[7]

Years later, when Abraham Lincoln took up the issue, the Civil War was
fought, and Jefferson's words were repeated in Lincoln's "Gettysburg
Address"; but the words came to mean something different: Negroes were
finally included too. Yet even until the 1940s, when *Native Son* was published, America still circumvented these words with the Jim Crow laws of
the South. In the introduction to *Native Son*, Wright explains:

> The Bigger Thomases were the only Negroes I know of who
> consistently violated the Jim Crow laws of the South and got
> away with it, at least for a sweet brief spell. Eventually, the
> whites who restricted their lives made them pay a terrible price.
> They were shot, hanged, maimed, lynched, and generally
> hounded until they were either dead or their spirits broken.[8]

These words of Wright proved true, not only in the South, but all over the
United States because Negroes continued to be scandalously tormented and
tempted by the promise of the American Dream: a chance for incredible op-
portunities, including equality, justice and financial success, which never became theirs because of oppression. Wright further explains in his introduction:

> He [Bigger] was an American, because he was a native son; but
> he was also a Negro nationalist in a vague sense because he was
> not allowed to live as an American. Such was his way of life
> and mine; neither Bigger nor I resided fully in either camp.
> (xxiv)

Ironically, the title of Wright's novel expresses the irony of a native son
who is nevertheless an outsider because he is black.
   Concerning the second characteristic of existentialist literature—the
common situations in which human freedom asserts itself—Wright, in what
seems a direct address to Hazel Barnes's criteria, says in his introduction:

> In a fundamental sense, an imaginative novel represents the
> merging of two extremes; it is an intensely intimate expression
> on the part of a consciousness couched in terms of the most ob-
> jective and commonly known events. It is at once something

private and public by its very nature and texture. Confounding
the author who is trying to lay his cards on the table is the dog-
ging knowledge that his imagination is a kind of community
medium of exchange: what he has read, felt, thought, seen, and
remembered is translated into extensions as impersonal as a
worn dollar bill. (vii)

Some pages later Wright goes on to say: "As I contemplated Bigger and
what he meant, I said to myself: 'I must write this novel, not only for others
to read, but to *free* [my emphasis] *myself* of this sense of shame and fear'"
(xxii). This basic situation of freedom—the free choice of freeing oneself
from fear and shame—is what characterizes existentialist literature. Camus
explains in *The Myth of Sisyphus* that if fear becomes "conscious of itself," it
is the most 'harrowing" passion ever experienced, turning into anguish; but
it is the perpetual landscape where the absurd human dwells "in whom
existence is concentrated."9

Killing Mary Dalton, Bigger's accidental victim, is an act of rebellion. He
has chosen to act and in that act, frees himself from the fear and shame thrust
upon him by a dominant white society that calls him a black "jungle beast"
and a "rapist" for trying to help this woman to her room, since she has
passed out from drinking. Bigger, like Orestes in Sartre's *The Flies*, learns to
accept the consequences of his murderous actions, as Sartre says all people
must. Yet Bigger comes into existence on a higher plane, obviously more
human, than he occupied previously because he no longer fears whites and
feels shame in their presence as he has during most of his life because of his
color. He accepts his actions because they make him feel free, give him the
possibility of choice, and provide for him an opportunity to feel that his actions carry weight. In other words, the common situation in which human
freedom affirms itself is obvious: if Bigger is kept in an inferior place and
made to live in bad faith, then he must be made to feel guilty, through shame
and fear, for the color of his skin. If he rejects this guilt, if he makes manifest
that he is alive through revolt and the death of others, then he must accept
total responsibility for his actions and balance this with his freedom.

The social implications of this novel, the final characteristic of existentialist literature, become manifest in the long speech Bigger's lawyer makes
on his client's behalf. Bigger becomes a living symbol of much that is rotten
in America: minority oppression. His lawyer poses the question of Bigger's
humanity in relation to all other Americans and, by implication, to all people
in the world. If a society presents ideals to which its people should aspire,
yet denies them any means of achieving them, then this society operates in

bad faith because it merely mocks these very same people. Stated in another way, if society preaches freedom for all, yet denies it to blacks, society's view of itself is false. If we do not respect the freedom of the Negroes, how can we respect ourselves? He states that if we multiply Bigger by twelve million, we have a separate nation of alienated individuals devoid of any social rights. The guilt is upon the nation's conscience.

In Sartre's "Portrait of an Antisemite," he tells us that anti-Semitic people are not afraid of Jews but of themselves, their freedom, and their conscience; essentially, anti-Semitic people or racists in general are cowards.[10] Similarly Wright suggests that since America has designated Negroes as not equal to whites, Negroes ought to reject this supposition; and he urges them to realize their freedom, cast off the yoke of their oppressors and rebel. Wright further suggests that only violence can provide people with any hope of dignity. During the trial, Max warns the courtroom that if Bigger has figured this out without much education, what will happen when millions do the same, rising in revolt. Consequently, Bigger stands for more than his personal situation by his acts of murder. He is the vanguard of a self-conscious movement toward liberation and creation.

Having established *Native Son's* connection with existentialist literature, I want to focus more on the way the absurd appears in the novel. In Donald Gibson's critique of *Native Son*, he says:

> The novel should be compared not only to *Crime and Punishment*, the work with which it is most frequently compared, but with *The Stranger* as well. Wright's and Camus's novels were published two years apart (1940 and 1942 respectively), and there are many striking parallels between them. (103)

Esther Jackson agrees:

> Interpreted in the forties primarily as a socio-political tract, *Native Son* may in the light of recent history—political and intellectual—be seen for its greatest merit: as a record of a man's dramatic encounter with Fate in the climate of the absurd. To be understood clearly, *Native Son* should be viewed in the light of other works in the contemporary genre. Like *Crime and Punishment*, or *The Stranger*, it is a study [...] of the absurd cycle [...].[11]

If the above is true, there must be parallels to *The Stranger* and by association *The Myth of Sisyphus* as well because these two works by Camus are analogous, as I have explained in CHAPTER IV.

Briefly stated, *Native Son* is the story about a young black man, Bigger Thomas, growing up in Chicago's Black Belt and trying to find an identity or some sense of self-understanding. The novel is divided into three sections. The first section, "Fear," traces Bigger's life from the time he wakes up and kills a big black rat in the squalid, one-room apartment he shares with his mother, sister, and brother to the time he creeps back in bed twenty-one hours later after killing a white girl, Mary Dalton, since he doesn't want to be caught in Mary's bedroom by her mother. She is the daughter of a prominent, rich family whom Bigger works for as a chauffeur, and they own the dilapidated tenement in which his family lives. Mr. Dalton is a supposed philanthropist for the blacks, and his wife is physically and socially blind.

The second part of the novel, "Flight," describes Bigger's awakening to life. Paradoxically, it occurs when his life is most in danger. For the first time in his life, he has done something in which he will know the consequences of his actions, and it makes him feel powerful and free. Armed with this knowledge, Bigger attempts to extort ransom money from the family under the pretense that Mary was kidnapped by a Communist group. His plans fail, and, as a result, he also kills his unwilling accomplice/mistress, Bessie, to keep her from giving him away to the police. This section ends with Bigger trying to flee, but he finally gets captured by the authorities.

The last section of the novel, "Fate," dovetails the three sections together by describing how all of society, both black and white, have had some part in his murderous actions. His lawyer, Boris Max, makes a genuine effort to help and understand Bigger, and it awakens within the black youth a vague sense of friendship between people. In the trial Max does his best to defend Bigger, but he is tried, found guilty, and sentenced to death. The story ends, much like *The Stranger*, as Bigger awaits his execution.

Besides the striking similarities between the endings of Camus's and Wright's novels, there is a brief scene at the beginning of *Native Son* which will suffice to show the connection between the two, pointing to the absurd. Bigger leaves his apartment to go to his new job as a chauffeur. Since he has a lot of spare time before he is due at the Dalton's home, he goes to the pool-room to see his friends. Standing outside with Gus, while waiting for the others to arrive in order to plan a robbery, Bigger wistfully looks up at a plane that is skywriting an advertisement. Gus remarks that the white boys sure can fly. Bigger responds that white people get a chance to do everything, and if he had the chance he could fly too. Gus laughs and makes fun of Bigger by telling him that if he wasn't black, if he had some money, and if they would let him into aviation school, then he could fly a plane. Bigger contemplates all the "ifs" and both men laugh heartily. Next, Bigger responds that it's "funny" how whites treat blacks, and Gus replies that "it better be funny." Bigger adds to the humor by saying maybe it's better he doesn't know how to fly because if he could, he would take some bombs up with him and drop them. They both laugh hysterically at this last remark.

Both the laughter and humor, in the scene mentioned above, set up the motif for the story as a whole. This episode is a symbolic rendering of the absurd world that Bigger lives in by depicting society's foibles, and it foreshadows his revolt, freedom and passion. In *The Myth of Sisyphus* Camus tells us that the absurd has a "comical aspect," defining it as something "contradictory" (29). Our absurd condition arises from the clash between ideal and reality, between what things are and the way they ought to be. What is so contradictory in Bigger's life that causes him to laugh? Bigger is living in the absurd world of "ifs"—the demands from the idealized image of himself—and he laughs because it is a passive activity of defense to prevent the upsurge of self-hate from a subhuman existence, reflecting the powerlessness and meaninglessness of his life. Bigger, like Camus's Meursault, is the phantom outsider. He is a metaphysical prisoner—a man trapped between concepts called black and white—and he lives in a gray area of abject poverty, overwhelming humiliation, and stifling frustration. The absurd for Bigger is the clash between the white world and his blackness, evoking that "divorce between man and his life, the actor and his setting," which causes alienation. Bigger's response to Gus after the skywriting plane passes and they "play white" is worth noting:

> Goddammit, look! We live here and they live there. We black
> and they white. They got things and we ain't. They do things
> and we can't. It's just like living in jail. Half the time I feel like
> I'm on the *outside* [my emphasis] of the world peeping in
> through a knot-hole in the fence.[12]

Bigger lives in a society that wants to keep the Negro in his place, not letting him soar like the skywriting plane which advertises a part of the American Dream. Because of the three "ifs," white society banishes him to the role of subordination and inferiority, restricts his freedom of movement, and discourages his ambition. The three "ifs" that Bigger and Gus laugh about, concerning their plight in life, give way to the three sections of the book—the three "F's" ("Fear," "Flight," and "Fate")—echoing familiar terms that the existentialists use quite frequently to describe the emotional intensity of a rootless person living in a world devoid of meaning. Wright further explains this idea in his introduction:

> What made Bigger's social consciousness most complex was the fact that he was hovering unwanted between two worlds— between powerful America and his own stunted place in life— and I took upon myself the task of trying to make the reader feel this No Man's Land . The most that I could say of Bigger was that he felt the *need* for a whole life and *acted* out of that need; that was all. (xxiv)

The notion of the absurd that Camus speaks of in *The Myth of Sisyphus*, concerning people "secreting the inhuman" and "this discomfort in the face of man's own inhumanity," takes specific form through Bigger's mother. Trying to coerce Bigger into accepting a job that the relief agency has offered him, so the family can continue to eat, his mother offers a bitter diatribe:

> Bigger, sometimes I wonder why I birthed you [...]. We wouldn't have to live in this garbage dump if you had any manhood in you [...]. He's just crazy [...]. Just plain dumb black crazy [...]. Bigger, honest, you the most no-countest man I ever seen in all my life [...]. Some of these days you going to wish you had made something out of yourself, instead of just a tramp. (11-13)

To avoid the absurd, Bigger initially lives in bad faith, refusing to acknowledge the reality of his life: "He knew that the moment he allowed what his life meant to enter fully into his consciousness, he would either kill himself or someone else" (14). This indicates that Bigger's fear is the fear of self-knowledge, which foreshadows the necessary change that Bigger must undergo if he is to make authentic existential choices. Living mechanically, the "why" that Camus speaks of in *The Myth of Sisyphus* does not enter into Bigger's consciousness at this time, because he is mostly unreflective about his life (much like Meursault in the first half of *The Stranger*). This becomes readily apparent from the opening pages of *Native Son*: "He was sick of his life at home. Day in and day out there was nothing but shouts and bickering. But what could he do? Each time he asked himself that question his mind hit a blank wall and he stopped thinking" (16). When anyone threatens to make him aware of the disappointments in his life, Bigger tries to "blot" them out of his mind, including himself: "He hated himself at that moment. Why was he acting and feeling this way? He wanted to wave his hand and blot out the white man who was making him feel like this. If not that, he wanted to blot himself out (49-50)."[13] This is similar to Camus's reverse analysis of the myth of Eurydice and how the absurd fades when we cease to acknowledge it. Bigger's reasoning is faulty and ineffective in the face of the emotional intensity evoked by the daily frustrations of his life.

With very little education, his capacity for reflection is limited and holds no priority for him. This idea is also reinforced in the first scene of the novel as Bigger kills a black rat that is running around the family's squalid apartment. Hitting the rat first with a skillet to stun it, Bigger takes a shoe and crushes the rat's head while "cursing hysterically: You sonofa*bitch.*" This destruction of the head (using Unamuno's terminology) is also significant in the murders of both Mary and Bessie and symbolic of a hostility toward the intellect. He first smothers Mary with a pillow over her head, and then decapitates her in the basement; to kill Bessie in the abandoned apartment building they have fled to, he repeatedly pounds her head in with a brick and throws her down an air-shaft.[14] In the dream Bigger has after he has killed Mary, he has also symbolically lost his head. This suggests a hatred of what he knows is undeveloped in himself but covered over by bad faith:

> [H]e had a big package in his arms so wet and slippery and heavy that he could scarcely hold onto it and he wanted to know what was in the package and he stopped near an alley corner and unwrapped it and the paper fell away and he saw—it was his own head [...]. (156)

Bigger's family situation, dominated by crowded physical space and lack of privacy, intensifies Sartre's account of the significance of the "look" in relationship to "shame."[15] Both male members of the family must look away in the morning while the women are getting dressed and vice versa because they live in a one-room, cage-like kitchenette on Chicago's South Side. The fear of being looked at (the shame of being objectified) is an inescapable, daily ritual. "The two boys kept their faces averted while their mother and sister put on enough clothes to keep them from feeling ashamed; and the mother and sister did the same while the boys dressed" (8). In such cramped quarters the Thomas family members (and by implication all blacks in segregated ghettos) are leading lives especially vulnerable to the "look": the "look" of the "Other" is inevitable and condemning. The alienation that

Negroes experience as others look at them is compounded (though not completely limited to this aspect) because of social oppression, not only from whites but Negroes too: "I told you not to look at me! Vera screamed. [...] Ma, make 'im [Bigger] stop looking at me, Vera wailed" (98).

Like all oppressed people, Bigger is taught from a young age that he lives apart from others. It is this lack of authentic, personal contact which creates the void in him because initially he lives daily and intensely the blacks' social role: the subhuman. Robert Bone explains:

> Living on the margin of his culture, Bigger is constantly tormented by the glitter of the dominant civilization. "The Gay Woman," a movie which he watches while waiting to rob a neighborhood store, is emblematic of that world of cocktail parties, golf, and spinning roulette wheels from which he is forever excluded. To fill the intolerable *void* [my emphasis] in his life he seeks "something big" [...].[16]

Not only does his family make him feel alienated with their gaze, but the white people he comes in contact with do the same. Some white people, professing a desire to know and help him, do so unknowingly with futile gestures of good will; Mary Dalton and Jan Erlone, her communist lover, are typical examples who, with their gaze, make Bigger feel that he is living in a strange and alien world:

> But they made him feel his black skin by just standing there looking at him, one holding his hand and the other smiling. He felt he had no physical existence at all right then; he was something he hated, the badge of shame which he knew was attached to a black skin. It was a shadowy region, a No Man's Land, the ground that separated the white world from the black that he stood upon. He felt naked, transparent; he felt that this white man, having helped to put him down, having helped to deform him, held him up now to look at him and be amused. (67-68)

The sense of being "Other" than the white world is as profound as the sense of being "Other" than nature itself. In Wright's notion of the absurd, the two seem to go hand in hand: "To Bigger and his kind white people were not really people; they were a sort of great natural force, like a stormy sky looming overhead, or like a deep swirling river stretching suddenly at one's feet in the dark" (109). In words Camus might have used in *The Myth of*

Sisyphus to describe the absurd in relationship to nature, Wright says in his introduction to *Native Son*:

> The feeling of looking at things with a painful and unwar-
> rantable nakedness was an experience, I learned, that tran-
> scended national and racial boundaries. It was this intolerable
> sense of feeling and understanding so much, and yet living on a
> plane of social reality where the look of a world which one did
> not make or own struck one with a blinding objectivity and tan-
> gibility [...]. (xvii)

While Meursault reacts to the force of the sun, Bigger is unnerved by the fiery furnace. Bigger's job, besides driving the Dalton family around town, is to go to the basement and tend the fire in the furnace by adding coal and disposing of the ashes that accumulate in the lower bin. After Bigger has killed Mary, he takes her body to the basement in order to dispose of it. Placing her corpse in the furnace, her head does not fit, so he chops it off with a hatchet he finds nearby. Fearing what he might find, Bigger never cleans out the ashes in the furnace:

> How about Mary? Had she burned? He turned the light on and
> picked up the piece of paper [...]. The inside of the furnace
> breathed and quivered in the grip of fiery coals [...]. The coals
> had the appearance of having burnt the body beneath, leaving
> the glowing embers formed into a shell of red hotness with a
> hollowed space in the center, keeping still in the embrace of the
> quivering coals the huddled shape of Mary's body [...]. As long
> as no one poked round in that fire, things would be all right. He
> himself did not want to poke it, for fear that some part of Mary
> was still there [...]. Maybe he ought to shake the ashes down?
> Yes. The fire must not become so clogged with cinders that it
> would not burn. At the moment he stooped to grasp the protrud-
> ing handle of the lower bin to shake it to and fro, a vivid image
> of Mary's face as he had seen it upon the bed in the blue light of
> the room gleamed at him from the smoldering embers and he
> rose abruptly, giddy and hysterical with guilt and fear. His
> hands twitched; he could not shake the ashes now. He had to get
> out into the air [...]. (112-14)

Ultimately, it is the fearful, hot, smoking furnace that leads to the discovery of Mary's remains by the reporters and causes Bigger's downfall. In retrospect, the three "ifs" that I spoke of earlier in regards to Bigger's oppressed life, give way to the three "F's" of each section—"Fear," "Flight," and "Fate"—and are all inextricably linked to the fiery furnace, which ties the three sections together; therefore, Bigger's fear of the fiery furnace inevitably leads to his flight and his capture which seals his fate. "The furnace which continually excites his fear to an intensity comparable to that responsible for his murder of Mary, is the curse or mistake that instigates Bigger's capture."[17]

Although Bigger avoids the heat from the furnace at this time, he does begin to confront the absurd through thought and action, not simply reacting emotionally. Subsequently, he successfully throws suspicion off of himself by telling everybody that Mary's lover, Jan Erlone, was the last person to see her. Since Jan is a known Communist, also an outsider, Bigger uses that fact to stage a kidnap scenario. He attempts to extort money from the rich Dalton family by delivering a note outlining Mary's capture by Communists and demanding a ransom of $10,000. Bigger's capacity for logical thinking comes alive for the first time in his life because he is moving from unreflective to reflective thinking. He is now able to make some authentic existential choices by passing from the realm of silence to that of understanding. As Gibson (98) notes, "The point is that Bigger, through introspection, finally arrives at a definition of self which is his own and different from that assigned to him by everyone else in the novel." Bigger's thoughts after he tells Bessie of the kidnap plot are significant:

> He felt that he had his destiny in his grasp. He was more alive than he could ever remember having been; his mind and attention were pointed, focused toward a goal. For the first time in his life he moved consciously between two sharply defined poles: he was *moving away* from the threatening penalty of death, from the death-like times that brought him that tightness and *hotness* [my emphasis because this relates to the heat of the sun as experienced by Meursault] in his chest; and he was moving toward that sense of fullness he had so often but inadequately felt in magazines and movies. (141)

This idea is reinforced if one considers Bigger's contrived reactions to other people. Not only does he implicate Jan as a suspect in a made-up kidnap plot, but he deceives the Daltons through his behavior as a stereotypic "nigger" (Bigger's name—a combination of "blind nigger" suggests this idea). As Bigger begins to see differently, his blindness to life is removed: he is learning to exploit the blindness of others. In fact, he is finally looking back:

> They did not want to see what others were doing if that doing did not feed their own desires. All one had to do was be bold, do something nobody thought of. The whole thing came to him in the form of a powerful and simple feeling; there was in everyone a great hunger to believe that made him blind, and if he could see while others were blind, then he could get what he wanted and never be caught at it. Now, who on earth would think that he, a black timid Negro boy, would murder and burn a rich white girl and would sit and wait for his breakfast like this? Elation filled him. (102)

Bigger's reactions to Britten, the private detective Mr. Dalton has hired to find Mary, poignantly depicts Bigger's heightened rational awareness and creative thinking. Bigger hides his intelligence from Britten by giving dumb answers to the detective's questions, fulfilling Britten's expectations of the stupidity and harmlessness of Negroes:

> "You *are* a Communist, you *goddamn* black sonofabitch! And you're going to tell me about Miss Dalton and that Jan bastard."
> "*Naw*suh! I ain't no Communist! *Naw*suh!" [...]
> Britten turned to Bigger and looked at him; Bigger kept his eyes down.
> "Boy, I just want to know, are you telling the truth?"
> "Yessuh, I'm telling the truth. I just started to work here last night. I ain't done nothing. I did just what they told me to do."
> "You sure he's all right?" Britten asked Dalton
> "He's all right." [...]
> "Go on to your room Bigger," said Mr. Dalton. [...]
> "I'm a little sorry you bothered him. He's here to try to get a new slant on things."
> Well, you see 'em one way and I see 'em another. To me, a nigger's a nigger." [...]
> "You got to be rough with 'em Dalton. See how I got that dope out of 'im? He wouldn't've told you that." (152-54)

As Bigger returns to his room he thinks of the kidnap note and how he "would show that Britten bastard." Also as he thinks about Mary's death and what it symbolizes, knowledge becomes a power equal to feeling in Bigger's life: "The knowledge that he killed a white girl they loved and regarded as their symbol of beauty made him feel the equal of them, like a man who had been somehow cheated, but had now evened the score" (155).

After killing Mary, Bigger experiences a sense of freedom (one of Camus's consequences of the absurd) because this is the first time any of his actions have had any worth and value in his life: "It was a kind of eagerness he felt, a confidence, a fullness, a freedom; his whole life was caught up in a supreme and meaningful act" (111). His profound urge for freedom becomes manifest in this spontaneous response to existence because he now voluntarily chooses his path in life. Once again, as Sartre notes:

> [F]irst of all, man exists, turns up, appears on the scene, and only afterwards defines himself. If man, as the existentialist conceives him, is indefinable, he is nothing. Only afterward will he be something, and he himself will have made what he will be.[18]

Back at the Dalton's home the next day after the murder, Bigger again reflects about this new freedom and its ramifications: "The mere thought that these avenues of action were open to him made him feel free, that his life was his, that he held his future in his hands" (179).

Later, during the trial, Max will echo these very same thoughts and feelings, initially evinced by Bigger, as the Jewish lawyer attempts to show Bigger's realization of freedom through murder: "He accepted it because it made him free, gave him the possibility of choice, of action, the opportunity to act and to feel that his actions carried weight" (364).

This newly found freedom symbolizes a partial liberty from the fear of being black, in the dominant white world in which he lives, because he has confronted his liberty for the first time on his own terms. Ultimately, Bigger will understand the meaning of his life from this particular action—the murder is gratuitous and absurd—and he will continue to murder to completely free himself of those blacks who remind and bind him to submissiveness and oppression: his mistress Bessie who is symbolic of the Sambo mentality. After Bigger kills Bessie (this is no accidental murder), to keep her from telling the police, he is absolutely free to think and feel as an existentially liberated person. Margolies (77) explains: "Bigger has *opted* to become a murderer, and freely chosen this identity. In an absurd, hostile world that

denies his humanity and dichotomizes his personality, he has made a choice
that somehow integrates his being." After killing Bessie, Bigger reflects long
and hard about his new place in the world and feels differently than before:

> But what was he after? What did he want? What did he love and
> what did he hate? He did not know. There was something he
> *knew* and something he *felt*; something the *world* gave him and
> something he *himself* had; something spread out in *front* of him
> and something spread out in *back*; and never in all his life, with
> this black skin of his, had the two worlds, thought and feeling,
> will and mind, aspiration and satisfaction, been together; never
> had he felt a sense of wholeness. (225)

Instead of blotting out his life, Bigger is now able to live fully and freely,
accepting whatever consequences come as the result of his actions:

> [T]hese two murders were the most meaningful things that had
> ever happened to him. He was living, truly and deeply, no mat-
> ter what others might think, looking at him with their blind
> eyes. Never had he had the chance to live out the consequences
> of his actions; never had his will been so free as in this night
> and day of fear and murder and flight. (225)

Bigger's murderous act is also described as one of creation. It is through
the clash between his intent and reality that this act becomes a reaction to his
absurd position in America. Bigger creates himself anew as he faces despair:

> The thought of what he had done, the awful horror of it, the dar-
> ing associated with such actions, formed for him for the first
> time in his fear-ridden life a barrier of protection between him
> and a world he feared. He had murdered and had created a new
> life for himself. It was something that was all his own, and it
> was the first time in his life he had anything that others could
> not take from him [...]. He was outside of his family now, over
> and beyond them; they were incapable of even thinking that he
> had done such a deed. (101)

As Bigger refashions his life through a creative act, the "crime" becomes "an
anchor weighing him safely in time," giving him an acute consciousness
(101). This is another of Camus's experiences of the absurd—the passage of

time—and this coincides with Camus's idea that "creating is living doubly."

This idea of creation as a meaningful force in relationship to time is very significant in *Native Son*. Once again Wright explains in his introduction:

> The more I thought of it the more I became convinced that if I did not write of Bigger as I saw and felt him, if I did not try to make him a living personality and at the same time a symbol of all the larger things I felt and saw in him, I'd be reacting as Bigger himself reacted: that is, I'd be acting out of *fear* if I let what I thought whites would say constrict and paralyze me [...]. In fact the novel, *as time passed* [my emphasis], grew upon me to the extent that it became a necessity to write it; the writing turned into a way of living for me. (xxi-xxii)

These words (reminiscent also of Unamuno and his yearning for more life through creativity) demonstrate that art is born in the quest for authentic existence against a meaningless world, linking time and creation with revolt. Camus explains that "creation" is our most effective way to express "patience and lucidity" (*Myth* 115) because it repeats and marks time, giving us dignity; it is also proof of our revolt against any dogma that puts a limit on our truth of experience in life.

During the trial, Max will tell the judge that Bigger's act of murder was also "an act of creation"; Max will explain this creative act in terms of revolt also and the impending doom in which millions of blacks will rise up and kill in order to be free:

> If that mob outdoors is afraid of *one* man, what will it feel if *millions* rise? How soon will someone speak the word that resentful millions will understand: the word to be, to act, to live? Is this Court so naïve as to think that they will not take a chance that is even less risky than Bigger Thomas took? (369)

Furthermore, Max will appeal to the judge's sense of self-realization (the judge will be the one to render the verdict and pass sentence), by linking Bigger's revolt to the American Revolutionary War:

> Your Honor, remember that men can starve from a lack of self-realization as much as they can from a lack of bread! And they can *murder* for it, too! Did we not build a nation, did we not wage war and conquer in the name of a dream to realize our

personalities and to make those realized personalities secure!
(366)

Continuing with other aspects of revolt, which relate to Bigger's metaphysical state, Camus says in *The Myth of Sisyphus* that since peril provides a person with a singular chance of grasping awareness, likewise "metaphysical revolt" extends that awareness to all of experience (*Myth* 54). In the introduction to the novel, Wright echoes Camus's words by explaining the lack of metaphysical meaning in Bigger's life which causes his revolt:

> [It was] a world whose fundamental assumptions could no longer be taken for granted: a world ridden with class and national strife, a world whose metaphysical meanings had vanished; [...] a world in which men could no longer retain their faith in an ultimate hereafter. It was a highly geared world whose nature was conflict and action, a world whose limited area and vision imperiously urged men to satisfy their organisms, a world that existed on a plane of animal sensation alone [...]. Speaking figuratively, they were soon chronic alcoholics, men who lived by violence, through extreme action and sensation, through drowning daily in a perpetual nervous agitation. (xix-xx)

Bigger's revolt is manifest not only in his murderous actions, but more importantly in the private conversation that he has with the State's Attorney, Mr. Buckley, before the trial. Buckley tries to pin other rapes and murders on Bigger which remain unsolved, but the black youth remains adamant and attempts to live in good faith by taking responsibility for only his rebellious actions: "I don't care what happens to me, but you can't make me say things about other people" (285). This is largely due to Bigger's acknowledgment of his rationality, even though Buckley tries to convince him that there is a possibility of an insanity plea and a chance for a loophole:

> "I once talked to a colored boy who raped and killed a woman, just like you raped and killed Mrs. Clinton's sister...."
> "I didn't do it!" Bigger screamed.
> "Why keep saying that? If you talk, maybe the judge'll help you. Confess it all and get it over with. You'll feel better. Say, listen, if you tell me everything, I'll see that you're sent to the hospital for an examination, see? If they say you're not *respon-*

sible [my emphasis], then maybe you won't have to die...."
    Bigger's anger rose. He was not crazy and he did not want to
be called crazy.
    "I don't want to go to no hospital."
    "It's a way out for you, boy."
    "I don't want no way out." (286-287)

As Bigger says these words, one can't help think of Sartre's play *No Exit* and
Inez's comment to Garcin, "You are your life, and nothing else."[19] Finally,
in words Unamuno might well have used to describe the tragic sense of life,
Wright leaves Bigger at the end of this scene on the floor crying: "He lay on
the cold floor sobbing; but really he was groping forward with fierce zeal
into a welter of circumstances which he felt contained a water of mercy for
the thirst of his head and heart" (288).
    Elsewhere in the novel, Bigger revolts against religion and its concomi-
tant passivity and guilt, unlike the rest of the characters in the novel. In a
scene reminiscent of *The Stranger*, Reverend Hammond comes into Bigger's
cell at the end of the novel to save the boy's soul. Bigger has thrown away
the wooden crucifix the preacher has given him because it reminds Bigger
not of the cross of Christ, but of the flaming wooden cross the Ku Klux Klan
has set on fire in Bigger's honor outside of the Dalton's home. Like
Meursault, Bigger physically threatens the reverend and sends the man
sprawling, slamming the cell door in Hammond's face. As a result Bigger
experiences the void and nothingness so important to the climate of the absurd:

> The preacher walked away. The guard followed. Bigger was
> alone. His emotions were so intense that he really saw and
> heard nothing. [...]
> Never again did he want to feel anything like hope. That was
> what was wrong; he had let that preacher talk to him until
> somewhere in him he had begun to feel that maybe something
> could happen. (315)

This passage, so characteristic of Camus's atheism too, typifies the meaningless world Bigger lives in. Bigger denies religion and asserts the human
condition.
    Finally, let us examine the notion of death, which, according to Camus, is
the final experience of the absurd. In an almost exact parallel to *The
Stranger*, Bigger is tried, convicted, and sentenced to death for all the wrong

reasons. On the one hand, the journalists think that Bigger had help from the Communists since "they feel that the plan of the murder and kidnapping was too elaborate to be the work of a Negro mind" (229). On the other hand, from Bessie's prophetic words "they'll say you raped her" (213), continuing with Bigger's speech to Max: "Naw, Mr. Max. I didn't [rape her]. But nobody'll believe me" (323), the prosecution tries to prove that Bigger did in fact rape Mary and, therefore, had to kill her afterwards to prevent her from telling anybody.

Facing death alone in jail, Bigger has rejected religion ("The Negro preacher who had given him the cross had come and he had driven him away" [382]); his family ("Forget me, Ma" [278]); his fellow prisoners ("'Ain't you the guy they got for that Dalton job?'[...] He did not want to talk to them" [316]); and other Negroes and oppressive whites ("He did not want to talk to whites because they were white and he did not want to talk to Negroes because he felt ashamed. His own would be too curious about him" [316]). Nothing seems to be left for him, so once again Bigger lapses into passivity. As a corollary, the skywriting airplane, which I referred to earlier, has once again foreshadowed Bigger's attempted "flight" from death and any hopes of attaining the American Dream. Furthermore, Bigger is fleeing from the myth of a black man caught in a white woman's bedroom, the concomitant accusal of rape by white society, and his inevitable execution in an electric chair. Buckley's words prove prophetic for Bigger's fate:

> There is but one answer! He planned to rape, to kill, to collect! He burned the body to get rid of evidences of *rape*! He took the trunk to the station to gain time in which to burn the body and prepare the kidnap note. He killed her because he *raped* her! Mind you, Your Honor, the central crime here is *rape*! Every action points toward that! [...] I demand, in the name of the people of this state, that this man die for these crimes! (377-78)

Wright's protagonist, like Meursault, has been attempting to flee death, symbolized by heat: the heat from the fiery furnace is also symbolic of the "heat" from the electric chair. Ultimately, confronted with death in the electric chair, Bigger attempts to find some personal values he can cling to:

> He would not mind dying now if he could only find out what this meant, what he was in relation to all the others that lived, and the earth upon which he stood. Was there some battle everybody was fighting, and he had missed it? And if he had

missed it, were not the whites to blame for it? Were they not the
ones to hate even now? Maybe. But he was not interested in
hating them now. He had to die. It was more important to him
to find out what this new tingling, this new elation, this new ex-
citement meant. (335-36)

Bigger is searching for something to make his impending execution meaningful to him on his own terms, other than the accusal of rape, since he does
state, "You can't make me do nothing but die" (312)! The denouement for
Bigger will be much the same as it was for Meursault: Bigger will realize the
value of personal friendship as did Meursault and his vision of Marie's face
on the wall.

In the final pages of the novel, Max comes to Bigger's cell to tell the
youth that the governor has not granted a stay of execution. Realizing that all
people feel alienated, the beginnings of friendship come to life for Bigger
when he understands that Max has authentically tried to help: "He had lived
outside of the lives of men. Their modes of communication, their symbols
and images, had been denied him. Yet Max had given him the faith that at
bottom all men lived as he lived and felt as he felt" (386). Max tells Bigger
to "die free," yet the lawyer tries to qualify Bigger's freedom in terms of
strength of numbers due to historical and socio-economical reasons. Bigger
responds: "Ah, I reckon I believe in myself.... I ain't got nothing else.... I got
to die" (391). At this point something seems to transform in Bigger, and he
wants to tell Max how he saw things: "I didn't want to kill!" Bigger shouted.
"But what I killed for, I *am*" (391-92)! This statement, analogous to
Roquentin's words "And I too, wanted to *be*,"[20] is a clear indication of
Bigger's existential revelation, relating to freedom, revolt, and passion.
These three consequences of the absurd demonstrate that no outside forces
are now responsible for Bigger's present thoughts, actions, and feelings.
Bigger chooses to face his death on his own terms, not those of Max. Yet
just as murder gives Bigger a sense of freedom and revolt, it also gives him a
sense of passionate guilt. As Jackson (134) notes, "It is for Bigger then, as it
has always been for the hero, this consciousness of his which is the access to
knowledge. Through his cycle of suffering and revolt, he comes at last to a
passion for life itself, to the threshold of meaning." This takes specific form
as Bigger starts to rant: "It must've been pretty deep in me to make me kill! I
must have felt it awful hard to murder [...]. What I killed for must've been
good" (392)!

Max does not understand Bigger's personal terms of death, and, recoiling
in horror, Max gropes for his hat "like a blind man" in order to leave. From

this act we can see that Max is not truly the friend Bigger has been seeking. The key relationship Bigger accepts is Jan Erlone's since we have found out earlier that Jan forgives Bigger for killing Mary and encourages Bigger to accept Max as his lawyer. Jan Erlone's name—Er-lone or a-lone—suggests that he is Bigger's only friend because Jan, accepting partial guilt in this whole affair, says he too was "kind of blind." We know this to be true because of Bigger's final words to Max: "Tell...Tell Mister...Tell Jan hello" (392). Bigger's hesitation as he corrects himself, from Mister to Jan, portrays Bigger's acceptance of a white man as a friend, resolving Bigger's personal black/white dichotomy. This reveals Bigger's moment of consciousness while facing the absurd because his dignity as a human being surfaces as he accepts the consequences for his actions and thus himself. Joseph Skerrett explains: "At the last Bigger speaks as a free man and equal human being not to Max, who can not, finally, look him in the eye, but to Jan. Jan has paid his dues, suffered, and learned to see Bigger as a human being."[21] In words Camus might have well used in *The Myth of Sisyphus* to describe the return of Sisyphus to his rock and the moment of absurd consciousness, Wright says of Bigger:

> Bigger understood that Jan was not holding him guilty for what he had done [...]. Jan had spoken a declaration of friendship that would make other white men hate him: a particle of white rock had detached itself from that looming mountain of white hate and had rolled down the slope, stopping still at his feet. The word had become flesh. For the first time in his life a white man became a human being to him; and the reality of Jan's humanity came in a stab of remorse: he had killed what this man loved and had hurt him. He saw Jan as though someone had performed an operation upon his eyes, or as though someone had snatched a deforming mask from Jan's face. (268)

Bigger does not go to the electric chair hating all white people. He acknowledges the friendship of Jan, but this friendship will be given to only those who have merited it through their personal actions, "not to superficial sympathizers, patronizing philanthropists, or bureaucratically arrogant radical sectarians."[22] Bigger reaffirms life by giving up his own for the lives he took. He has found some type of human dignity, which is his own, and he does not fear being dragged to the electric chair; for he will be able to walk on his own. It is no mistake that Bigger repeatedly tells Max: "I'm all right."

This novel is absurdist, not only because of its affinities to *The Stranger*, but also because of its likeness to *The Myth of Sisyphus*. At the end of Camus's essay on the absurd, he says that revolt, freedom, and passion make up our greatest attributes because these consequences of the absurd give us an attitude similar to that of a conqueror: when the emotions and the intellect finally coexist, checking and balancing each other, it gives a person strength because it reveals an internal fortitude which gives shape to life and enables a person to create a work of art. These ideas by Camus can be compared to Wright's reasons for writing *Native Son*. Again in his introduction to this novel Wright states:

> And then, while writing, a new and thrilling relationship would spring up under the drive of emotion, coalescing and telescoping alien facts into a known and felt truth. That was the deep fun of the job: to feel within my body that I was pushing out to new areas of feeling, strange landmarks of emotion, tramping upon foreign soil, compounding new relationships of perceptions, making new and—until that very split second of time!—unheard-of and unfelt effects with words. It had a buoying and tonic impact upon me; my senses would strain and seek for more and more of such relationships; my temperature would rise as I worked. That is writing as I feel it, a kind of significant living. (xxx)

A few pages later Wright goes on to say:

> I don't know if *Native Son* is a good book or a bad book. And I don't know if the book I'm working on now will be a good book or a bad book. And I really don't care. The mere writing of it will be more fun and a deeper satisfaction than any praise or blame from anybody. (xxxiv)

If Bigger's murderous act was one of creation in which his freedom, revolt, and passion sprung forth, then likewise Wright's creation of this novel did the same for him. Wright has shaped and revealed the Negro's experience of the absurd: how blacks relate to one another and white people as well, their shared experiences in their struggles, triumphs, and defeats (spoken or unspoken), and their creation of a personal mode of existence. Irving Howe once stated that "the day *Native Son* appeared, American culture was changed forever."[23] This is because Wright, like Sisyphus, Meursault, and Bigger, all stubbornly challenged any system or authority that wanted to keep them in their place, thus creating their own forms of self-realization in confrontation with the absurd. Wright and his protagonist both move from obscurity to recognition through shared experiences in life. Bigger scorns the oppressive whites and submissive blacks as Sisyphus scorns the Gods. Wright's epigraph for this novel, from the Book of Job, supports this idea: "Even today is my complaint rebellious, / My stroke is heavier than my groaning."

NOTES

[1] Donald Gibson, "Wright's Invisible Native Son," *Twentieth Century Interpretations of Native Son*, ed. Houston Baker (Englewood Cliffs, N. J.: Prentice-Hall Inc., 1972) 107.

[2] Richard Macksey and Frank Moorer, "Introduction," *Richard Wright: A Collection of Critical Essays* (Englewood Cliffs, N. J.: Prentice-Hall Inc., 1984) 15.

[3] Robert Bone, *Richard Wright* (Minneapolis: Minnesota UP, 1969) 31.

[4] Edward Margolies, *Native Sons: A Critical Study of Twentieth-Century Negro American Authors* (Philadelphia and New York: J. B. Lippincott Co., 1968) 68.

[5] Hazel Barnes, *Humanistic Existentialism* (Lincoln: Nebraska UP, 1956) 15.

[6] Constance Webb, *Richard Wright: A Biography* (New York: G. P. Putnam's Sons, 1968) 261.

[7] Dorothy Fisher, "Introduction to the First Edition," *Twentieth Century Interpretations of Native Son*, ed. Houston Baker (Englewood Cliffs, N. J.: Prentice-Hall Inc., 1972) 110.

[8] Richard Wright, introduction, "How 'Bigger' Was Born," *Native Son* (New York and Evanston: Harper & Row, 1940) xi.

[9] Albert Camus, *The Myth of Sisyphus and Other Essays*, trans. Justin O'Brien (New York: Alfred Knopf, 1975) 22-24.

[10] Jean-Paul Sartre, "Portrait of an Antisemite," *Existentialism: From Dostoevsky to Sartre*, ed. Walter Kaufmann (New York: New American Library, 1975) 345.

[11] Esther Jackson, "The American Negro and the Image of the Absurd," *Richard Wright: A Collection of Critical Essays*, ed. Richard Macksey and Frank Moorer (Englewood Cliffs, N. J.: Prentice-Hall Inc., 1984) 131.

[12] Richard Wright, *Native Son* (New York and Evanston: Harper & Row, 1940) 23. In further references to this work in CHAPTER V, I will use page numbers only.

NOTES

13 See also pp. 95, 109, 128, 133, 275, 307, 386.

14 Dan McCall, "The Bad Nigger," *Twentieth Century Interpretations of Native Son*, ed. Houston Baker (Englewood Cliffs, N. J.: Prentice-Hall Inc., 1972) 82-83.

15 Jean-Paul Sartre, *Being and Nothingness*, trans. Hazel Barnes (New York: Philosophical Library, 1956) 261.

16 Robert Bone, "Richard Wright," *Twentieth Century Interpretations of Native Son*, ed. Houston Baker (Englewood Cliffs, N. J.: Prentice-Hall Inc., 1972) 76.

17 Joyce Ann Joyce, "The Tragic Hero," *Modern Critical Interpretations: Richard Wright's Native Son*, ed. Harold Bloom (New York: Chelsea House Publishers, 1988) 77.

18 Jean-Paul Sartre, "The Humanism of Existentialism," *Essays in Existentialism*, ed. Wade Baskin (Secaucus, N. J.: Citadel Press, 1965) 35-36.

19 Jean-Paul Sartre, *No Exit and Three Other Plays*, trans. Stuart Gilbert (New York: Vintage Books, 1955) 45.

20 Jean-Paul Sartre, *Nausea*, trans. Lloyd Alexander (New York: New Directions Publishing Corp., 1964) 175.

21 Joseph Skerrett, *Modern Critical Interpretations: Richard Wright's Native Son* (New York: Chelsea House Publishers, 1988) 142.

22 Paul Siegel, "The Conclusion of Richard Wright's *Native Son*," *Twentieth Century Interpretations of Native Son*, ed. Houston Baker (Englewood Cliffs, N. J.: Prentice-Hall Inc., 1972) 115.

23 Irving Howe, "Black Boys and Native Sons," *Twentieth Century Interpretations of Native Son*, ed. Houston Baker (Englewood Cliffs, N. J.: Prentice-Hall Inc., 1972) 63.

CHAPTER VI

THE LAST GENTLEMAN

My final example in this study of the absurd is *The Last Gentleman* by Walker Percy. Published in 1966, this novel was nominated for the National Book Award, and received critical acclaim for the characterization of a Southern gentleman, Will Barrett. Authors frequently write from their roots, and this novel is certainly no exception. Percy was a Southerner with a distinguished family heritage traceable back to 1776; however, this didn't prevent several of Percy's ancestors from committing suicide, including his father.[1] Consequently, suicide becomes a major theme in *The Last Gentleman*, like *The Myth of Sisyphus*. Yet Percy's novel reflects not only a growing, individual alienation and lack of possibility which leads some people to suicide, but a cultural degeneration in the modern world as well. To combat this alienation, Percy moves from the "I" to the "we" in this novel.

In *The Myth of Sisyphus*, after describing the various experiences of the absurd, Camus says:

> Let me repeat: all this has been said over and over. I am limiting myself here to making a rapid classification and to pointing out these obvious themes. They run through all literatures and all philosophies. [...] But it is essential to be sure of these facts in order to be able to question oneself subsequently on the primordial question. I am interested—let me repeat again—not so much in absurd discoveries as in their consequences. If one is assured of these facts, what is one to conclude, how far is one to

go to elude nothing? Is one to die voluntarily or to hope in spite
of everything?[2]

According to the above, the "obvious themes" and "resulting consequences"
are the important things to look for in determining what an absurdist novel
signifies and whether it gives us hope or leads us to suicide. Applying
Camus's notions, feelings, and consequences of the absurd from the aforementioned essay should afford good results in interpreting *The Last
Gentleman*.

Briefly stated, *The Last Gentleman* is a story about an unusual young
man, Will Barrett, who is a displaced 25-year-old Southerner living in New
York City. Overwhelmed by "everydayness,"[3] he lives at the Y.M.C.A. and
is employed as a humidification engineer (a janitor) in the basement at
Macy's. He has dropped out of school and, due to a nervous condition,
seems to be haunted by his own existence. Trying to resolve his problems in
the modern world, he seeks help through psychoanalysis, spending much
time and money on this endeavor over a period of five years. He does, by
chance, attach himself to a Southern family, the Vaughts, while they are in
New York, seeking medical help for their younger son, Jamie, who is dying
of leukemia. As a result of Will's interactions with this family, he asks their
youngest daughter, Kitty, to marry him, and he becomes mysteriously drawn
to their oldest son, Sutter, who is a gifted physician who Will thinks can help
him with his physical and mental condition. Will follows the family back to
Alabama and attempts to construct a relationship with them. In the end of
the novel, Sutter takes Jamie to the Southwest, so the young teenager can die
with dignity. Will follows the two males to the Southwest and comforts
Jamie; but Will must now make a choice and stop being simply an observer
in life, because after Jamie dies, Sutter wants to commit suicide. Based on
this brief summary, the question can be raised as to whether this work can be
described as an existentialist novel.

Returning again to Hazel Barnes's three characteristics of the literature of
humanistic existentialism,[4] we find that this story does work with myth.
Like the adventures of Odysseus, the story of Will Barrett, moving from
place to place, is the myth of travel and return. Percy explains travel
("rotation") in his essay "The Man on the Train" as a means of coping with
alienation due to everydayness:

> The road is better than the inn, said Cervantes—and by this he
> meant that rotation is better than the alienation of everydayness.
> The best part of Huckleberry Finn begins when Huck escapes

from his old man's shack and ends when he leaves the river for good at Phelps farm.[5]

By return, I mean a return to the past, and Percy calls this return a form of "repetition" ("Train" 95-100). In this novel, Will must go back home and discover what has caused his nervous condition, so he can proceed with his life. Will travels from New York City in the Empire State, which looks "bombed out" because it is located at "ground zero," to the Mississippi Delta in the South: "Moreover, suggestible as he was, he began to think it mightn't be a bad idea to return to the South and discover his identity, to use Dr. Gamow's expression."[6] This last phrase by Dr. Gamow suggests a limit to Will's success in the South, because Will is relying on another person to give him direction in life instead of himself. Will must travel Southwest to New Mexico, where "the atmosphere is a great deal clearer" and free from the "noxious" and "ravenous particles" in New York City. Will is embarking upon a journey of self-discovery. Martin Luschei explains: "Will's return to the South is a vital part of the Return, as Percy calls it, the search for an answer to the question, who am I?"[7]

Will travels about in a Trav-L-Aire camper nicknamed "Ulysses"; and "he was meant to lead us beyond the borders of the Western world and bring us home" (81-82). Looking the vehicle over, Will reflects about the uniqueness of Ulysses which is "in the world yet not of the world," and it is frequently referred to in nautical terms: on his way South, the camper "pushed like a boat" through the "heavy mothering air," arriving at the "Ur-plain" on the "alluvial floor" of the Mississippi "Delta" (124; 238-39). Furthermore, Will's hometown in the South is "Ithaca," located deep in the Mississippi Delta, where he must return in order to rediscover his past.

As an aid Will carries with him a telescope which he believes has "magical properties [...]. It had to do with its being German, with fabled German craftsmen, gnomic slow-handed old men in the Harz Mountains. These lenses did not merely transmit light. They penetrated to the heart of things" (31). (The play on words of Harz and heart reveals the telescope's primary function.) Also, "the telescope created its own world in the brilliant theater of its lenses" (12). It is from the use of this telescope, reminiscent of the "look" in existentialist literature,[8] that he sees and immediately falls in love with Kitty in Central Park. From this chance encounter, Percy says of Will:

[H]is heart gave a leap. He fell in love, at first sight and at a distance of two thousand feet. It was not so much her good looks

[...] as a certain bemused and dry-eyed expression in which he
seemed to recognize—himself! [...] She was his better half. (14)

Following up on her activities, through the telescope, he finally meets
and becomes involved with the entire Vaught family; next, he travels South
with them to their home in Alabama, and he becomes a "special sort of person" to each family member. This is especially true for Will because he possesses an "amiable Southern radar"; as a consequence of this unique ability,
he tunes "onto the wave lengths" of most people: "[T]he sentient engineer,
whose sole gift, after all, was the knack of divining persons and situations"
(46).

The Vaught's house on the golf links is described as a "castle [...] made
of purplish bricks which had been broken in two and the jagged side turned
out. It had beam-in-plaster gables and a fat Norman tower and casement
windows with panes of bottle glass" (152). Wandering around in the attic of
this house, Will begins his voyage into the past, trying to discover himself:
he once heard a shotgun blast coming from an attic, and this sparks forgotten
memories.

Finally, two objects—an Esso map and a casebook—left for him by
Sutter, tell "him where to go." These two aids help Will to chart his course
in order to find the teenager and the doctor. This journey, which can also be
seen as a quest for self-realization, makes clear to him, through authentic
actions, what his life means. Will is the long defunct Southern gentleman-
hero: his first name symbolizes his persistence in life; and the combination
of his first and last name plays on the words *will bear it*, suggesting a parallel to Camus's *The Stranger* with his insistence that Meursault is "the only
Christ we deserve."[9] This will be explained at the denouement of Percy's
novel.

Returning to Hazel Barnes's second characteristic—the common situations in which human freedom asserts itself—we find that Will, unlike his
father, resists the temptation to suicide. As Mary Howland notes, "Having
finally remembered his father's suicide, Will is freed from the past by his
own acknowledgment that his father was wrong to choose death."[10] Luschei
(155) agrees: "He has come back to Ithaca because he must fathom the
meaning of his father's suicide and somehow deal with it before he can be
free to become himself. His amnesia and even his deafness are related to
what he is blocking out." Trying to free himself from the past, "since his
family had turned ironical and lost its gift for action"(16), Will must actively
seek his life in a world rife with alienation and ambiguity; he must accept the
freedom to develop himself by "stepping down from the zone of the possible

to the zone of the realized" (30). Hence Will moves from the mode of pure possibility, which has no actuality and atrophies his ability to act, to that of human choice. At the beginning of the novel, he felt that "he had to know everything before he could do anything," rendering him immobile: the need to "know" is why he avoids decisions. As a point of reference, the character of Will could very well have developed from a description in one of Percy's earlier essays: "Who is he, this Gary Cooper person who manages so well to betray nothing of himself whatsoever, who is he but I myself, the locus of pure possibility" ("Train" 94). In Will's case, a chance encounter with a woman, Kitty, allows him to fall in love and create himself anew:

> For until this moment he had lived in a state of pure possibility, not knowing what sort of a man he was or what he must do, and supposing therefore that he must be all men and do everything. But after this morning's incident his life took a turn in a particular direction. Thereafter he came to see that he was not destined to do everything but only one or two things. (11-12)

Jerome Taylor clarifies this point:

> A person, then, is aroused to action by the call of things that come upon him: persons, events, demands for responsible decision. As Marcel puts it, "You invite me to create myself. You are this very invitation." This invitation to a self-creating act is essentially what happened when [...] Will sees Kitty through the telescope and falls in love with her.[11]

By the end of the novel Will has discovered that although the past is fixed, one's relation to it or how one views it can be changed. This is a good example of Sartre's claim that we can spontaneously change our fundamental project, and so, all our values and meanings. This is an expression of Will's freedom: "This is the locus of pure possibility, he thought, his neck prickling. What a man can be the next minute bears no relation to what he is or what he was the minute before" (278). Coming to terms with his past, Will experiences the initial stage of self-actualization.

It is this sense of freedom which enables Will to find out who he is. At the beginning of the novel while using his telescope, Will is merely an observer; he has difficulty choosing, and his freedom is limited at this time: "Even now he made the highest possible scores on psychological aptitude tests, especially in the area of problem-solving and goal seeking. The trouble was he couldn't think what to do between tests" (15). Subsequently, he must learn to take some form of positive action, not simply be a voyeur in life, but seek things in life using the heart as well as the head (Unamuno's terminology) in order to realize a more complete freedom. Plainly, Will needs to separate abstract science from concrete experience, which means he must not sacrifice human authenticity. It is no mistake that Will is referred to as "the engineer":

> I am indeed an engineer, he thought, if only a humidification engineer, which is no great shakes of a profession. But I am also an engineer in a deeper sense: I shall engineer the future of my life according to the scientific principles and self-knowledge I have so arduously gained from five years of analysis. (39)

Luschei explains:

> In assigning Will Barrett, here in this euphoric state at the end of the first chapter, his permanent designation of engineer, Percy suggests his failing: he wants to *engineer* his life on the soundest "scientific" principles rather than to commit himself to the vexations and sovereign task of living it. (*Wayfarer* 125)

Will's alienation stems from the boredom and anxiety of "everydayness," and the "why" that Camus speaks of in *The Myth of Sisyphus*, regarding mechanical living, will loom up as Will realizes his freedom to choose. This will come from Sutter's post-hypnotic suggestion: "Now I shall not tell you what to do, but I will tell you now that you will be free to act" (214).

Will becomes open and free to new ways of living, exemplifying another of Camus's consequences of the absurd—"the pure flame of life"—which emphasizes Will's passion for the spontaneous:

> If a total stranger had stopped him this morning on Columbus Circle and thrust into his palm a note which read: *Meet me on the NE corner of Lindell Blvd and Kings Highway in St. Louis 9 A.M. next Thursday—have news of the utmost importance*, he'd have struck out for St. Louis (the question is, how many people nowadays would not?). (13)

Reminiscent of Dostoevsky's Underground Man, Will works in the

basement of Macy's at the beginning of the novel, but he emerges and lives
authentically as the novel progresses. At first, Will is contrary: "He felt bad
when other people felt good and good when they felt bad" (25); but he resolves to straighten his life out: "You do things by doing things, not by not
doing them. No more crazy upsidedownness, he resolved" (76). Like
Meursault, Will battles his problems of contemporary life head-on: Will is
adaptable and tells the truth. It is no mistake that he is also referred to as a
sentient, prudent, and puissant man throughout the book.

Regarding Hazel Barnes's final characteristic of existentialist literature—
social responsibility—we find throughout the novel that Will possesses
disponibilité.[12] As Robert Coles notes,

> Barrett is amiable, funny, charming; and at all times he seems
> *available* [my emphasis]—the man who has freed himself of
> obligations, and so is able to look at the world with the least
> number of reservations or prior (and inhibiting) commit-
> ments.[13]

Although he suffers from a nervous condition—amnesia, fugue states, gaps,
deafness in one ear, and a jerking knee—Will knows one thing for sure: "[I]t
is people who count, one's relations with people, one's warmth toward and
understanding of people" (17). Since Will is initially out of touch with his
own being, living an objective and scientific life, he is all openness and
availability for others. In other words, Will is chameleon-like: lacking an
internal life, he lives externally by accepting outside influences. As Will's
relationship with Kitty develops, wanting to "marry him a wife and live him
a life," he instinctively attaches himself to the entire Vaught family. Mr.
Vaught, seeing the change in Jamie's behavior in response to Will's availability and compassion for the family, wants to hire Will as a companion for
his ill-fated son. Jamie agrees:

> "Did Poppy speak to you?" he whispered.
> "Yes."
> "What did you say?"
> "We didn't get down to terms."
> "That's Poppy. But what do you say in general?"
> "I say O.K., if I can be of use to you." (75)

Likewise, Will makes himself available to all people with whom he
comes into contact; humble and caring, he is quick to notice foolish bravado

and pretense, yet he responds with tact and deference to people in need. The above relates to the subplot of the story: Will and Sutter's relationship. Before and after Jamie's death, Will takes it upon himself to discourage Sutter from committing suicide; this issue relates to Camus's primary and initial concern in *The Myth of Sisyphus* that the only important philosophical problem in life centers upon suicide. Will is attracted to Sutter, "seeing in Sutter a father who might have answers for him" (Lawson 33). As Will reads Sutter's casebook, he discovers much about the troubled doctor:

> Here is what happened. I became depressed last summer when I first saw Jamie's blood smear [...]. Went to ranch, shot myself, missed brain, carried away cheek. [...] I saw something clearly while I had no cheek and grinned like a skeleton. But I got well and forgot what it was. I won't miss next time. (291-92)

Right before Jamie dies, Sutter tells Will pointedly that he will kill himself a few hours after his brother's death. Consequently, the theme of intersubjectivity is developed by Percy as a positive alternative to suicide. From Will and Sutter's bond together, because of Jamie's death, a sense of social responsibility is manifest where caring for the other person affirms that two people can share the world together. Through the perception of Sutter's despair, which is akin to Will's own because of his father's death, Will is enabled to act accordingly: to overcome the human condition of loneliness through a bond with the other. Like all the novels I have discussed thus far, it is the theme of a one-on-one relationship that allows some form of passion for the other. Subsequently, Will lets people be who they are and then responds to them accordingly, unless death is imminent, in which case "he "refuses to accept the judgments others make on themselves as the final word" (Coles 188).

Will's nervous condition—amnesia, fugue states, and gaps—provides the initial parallel to *The Myth of Sisyphus*, and, in fact, Percy does admit a certain influence by Camus.[14] Camus's description of mechanical living and the passage of time are described by Percy as "everydayness": "the quest for the new as the new, the reposing of all hope in what my be around the bend" ("Train" 84-85). Both authors describe the notion of alienation that one may experience from day to day in these similar terms, and both suggest several ways to combat this feeling. In "The Man on the Train" Percy says that "rotation" is superior to "the alienation of everydayness" (89); and "amnesia is the one, the only, the perfect rotation" (92). Since the present is alienation for Will, he seeks possible adventures in the future which will combat this alienation; hence his amnesia is rooted in a past he wishes to deny and a future he continually lives for, thus partially living in bad faith because he does not confront the absurd which, "unlike Eurydice, [...] dies when we turn away from it." It is not by chance that Will wakes up from his fugue states and finds himself wandering around old battlefields in the South: "The summer before, he had fallen into a fugue state and wandered around northern Virginia for three weeks, where he sat sunk in thought on old battlegrounds, hardly aware of his own name" (18). At the beginning of the novel, we know that Will's father, Ed Barrett, is dead, but we do not know how he died. Later we find out that Ed had committed suicide, because, lacking possibility due to his stoic nature, he could not cope with the despair of everydayness. In words Camus might have used to describe the alienation which comes from a mechanical life, Percy says of Will's father:

> The father was a brave man too and he said he didn't care what others thought, but he did care. [...] He became ironical. For him it was not a small thing to walk down the street on an ordinary September morning. In the end he was killed by his own irony and sadness and by the strain of living out an ordinary day in a perfect dance of honor. (16)

Will also experiences this familiar alienation, so reminiscent of Meursault living through an ordinary Sunday.[15] Percy often gives us hints concerning Will's fear of time: "Yet it was on just such a day as this, an ordinary Wednesday or Thursday, that he felt the deepest foreboding. [...] It was not the prospect of the Last Day which depressed him but rather the prospect of living through an ordinary Wednesday morning" (25-26). Will constantly muses on these very same thoughts: "[M]y problem is how to live from one ordinary minute to the next on a Wednesday afternoon" (277).

To cope with boredom, Will unknowingly employs the rotation method and becomes pure transcendence in an existential mode in order to shut off his father's death. Sutter's casebook, which Will reads and memorizes, reinforces this idea:

> He wishes to cling to his transcendence and to locate a fellow transcender (e.g. me) who will tell him how to traffic with immanence (e.g., "environment," "groups," "experience," etc.) in such a way that he will be happy. [...]. [H]is posture is self-defeating. (276)

Yet Will's amnesia is the perfect escape from everydayness, enabling him to see things differently by reveling in the newness of the situation, much like Meursault and his relationship with Raymond or Marie (although Meursault isn't amnesic):

> To be specific, he had now a nervous condition and suffered spells of amnesia [...]. Much of the time he was like a man who has just crawled out of a bombed building. Everything looked strange. Such a predicament, however, is not altogether a bad thing. Like the sole survivor of a bombed building, he had no secondhand opinions and he could see things afresh. (17)

Percy confirms this idea in an interview with Ashley Brown, saying that "his [Will's] amnesia allows him to be a blank tablet [...]. Barrett's amnesia suggests a post-Christian shakiness about historic time" (Lawson and Kramer eds. 13). Also in this interview, Percy suggests that Will's amnesia is a factor in his homelessness in New York City and the reason he works underground: "Anyway, his transplantation to New York City causes him to have a temporal dislocation, and working in Macy's sub-basement at night doesn't help things. He becomes almost Oriental in his abstraction from time" (13).

As a corollary to the amnesia, Will is completely absorbed into groups: "As a consequence this young man, dislocated to begin with, hardly knew who he was from one day to the next. There were times when he took roles so successfully that he left off being who he was and became someone else" (23). Since Will's life is pure possibility, an abstraction of what other people want him to be and do, he loses his gift for authentic action because his amnesia allows him to escape without remembering. In *The Myth of Sisyphus*, Camus makes a similar point: "Tomorrow, he was longing for tomorrow, whereas everything in him ought to reject it" (*Myth* 14). Will's revolt of the flesh takes specific form through amnesia, because he is living for each successive moment but blotting out the past. In this instance, Percy is suggesting the ill effects that mass society has on the individual. Taylor explains:

> In his presentation of Will, Percy has, of course, purposely exaggerated to show his view of how science and a mass society have affected the consciousness of modern people. He embodies in his fictional characters various forms taken by the perennial "sickness unto death" in present-day Western culture. (*Search* 47)

Will's dislocation in New York City is inherent in his alienation, relating to his amnesia and reflecting the absurd: "It was possible for him to be at home in the North because the North was homeless. There are many things worse than being homeless in a homeless place—in fact, this is one condition of being at home, if you are yourself homeless" (149). In words Camus might have used to describe how "nature or a landscape can negate us," Percy, in the essay "The Message in the Bottle," describes the solitary and bewildering human condition as that of a person, like Will, being cast upon on an island, from the position of an outsider:

> But how does he know he is sick, let alone homesick? He may not know. He may live and die as an islander at home on his island. But if he does know, he knows for the simple reason that in his heart of hearts he can never forget who he is: that he is a stranger, a castaway, who despite a lifetime of striving to be at home on the island is as homeless now as he was the first day he found himself cast up on the beach.16

This idea is reinforced in an interview Percy gave to Carlton Creemens: "Man is alienated by the nature of his being here. He is here as a stranger and as a pilgrim, which is the way alienation is conceived in my books" (Lawson and Kramer eds. 28-29). Although Will is not surrounded by water, he is adrift in cities like New York with smog (ravenous and noxious particles) and open spaces with clean air (New Mexico). He is Percy's pilgrim-stranger. Hence Will develops a theory of "good and bad environments" and decides to move out of New York City. Again Percy defines Will in an essay and suggests why a man might go to New Mexico from New York: "To the alienated man of the East who has rotated to Santa Fe, the green shade of home becomes the true rotation" ("Train" 94).

Everydayness and homelessness suggest a loss of identity that is rooted in the past which must be confronted by Will, so he may live fully. Will's rotation of living for each successive moment does intensify his passion for life, allowing him to make himself available to others; and Camus says passion is one of the consequences of the absurd which is a desire to exhaust everything that is presently given and to treat the future indifferently.

In order to discover himself, Will must leave the Empire State and go South with the Vaught family, who draw him closer to his roots and his denied past. Will's past can be seen through Percy's idea of repetition, which has affinities with Camus's idea of time. In "The Man on the Train" Percy explains repetition:

> Repetition is the conversion of rotation. In rotation, Shane cannot stay. In repetition, Shane neither moves on or stays, but turns back to carry the search into his own past [...]. Like rotation, repetition offers itself as a deliverance from everydayness, yet it is, in a sense, the reverse of rotation. ("Train" 96)

If the above is true, Will must travel South to Ithaca and confront the past that he has so mysteriously forgotten. Will's father had committed suicide with a shotgun while Will was a boy, and the deafness in Will's right ear is a result of the concussion from the shotgun blast. Another part of Will's nervous condition is a series of *déjà vus* and flashbacks, relating to his father's suicide, which become increasingly concrete as he travels further South with the Vaught family, until he finally remembers the entire incident. Standing in front of his old house, he remembers it all. Percy says that one must "stand before the house of one's childhood" in order to recover himself or herself, "without surrendering the self as a locus of experience and possibility" ("Train" 95-96). (Percy's idea of repetition also reminds us of Sartre's comment in *Nausea* that "you don't put your past in your pocket; you have to have a house."[17])

In retrospect, the fatal incident happened one evening while Will was a boy: sitting on the porch steps, Will is minding the "Philco," which is clanking, whirring, and plopping "down the old 78's." "The Great Horn Theme" by Brahms is playing on the record player while his father is pacing up and down, under the "water oaks," in front of the house. Ed, frustrated and nervous, has been battling with the Ku Klux Klan, and he has a moment of self-discovery, realizing that he is too idealistic, that the social and moral codes of the nineteenth century have vanished. Panthea Broughton explains:

> He [Ed] committed suicide because his life could be redeemed only by a set of principles which, he discovered, were no longer in the world. The suicide then was for him a logical extension of the recognition that he and all he lived for were "out of it."[18]

The boy tries to tell his dad that he has won, since the KKK has left town; but Ed says:

> "Once they were the fornicators and the bribers and the takers of bribes and we were not and that was why they hated us. Now we are like them, so why should they stay? They know they don't have to kill me."

"How do they know that, Father?"
"Because we've lost it all, son."
"Lost what?"
"But there's one thing they don't know."
"What's that, Father?"
"They may have won, but I don't have to choose that."
"Choose what?"
"Choose them." (258-59)

With these final words Will's father turns to leave and Will calls out to him, "Wait. [...] Don't leave." The father responds that he is not leaving, but lies to the boy, goes inside the house, picks up the shotgun, enters the attic, fits the "muzzle of the Greener into the notch of his breastbone," and pulls the trigger. Ed's nineteenth-century romanticism, symbolized by the Brahms's music, has proved "nugatory," and he has "problems with transcendence and with returning to the immanent world" (Howland 59). Camus describes this position in regard to Dostoevsky's Kirilov: "This suicide kills himself because, on the metaphysical plane, he is *vexed*. In a certain sense he is taking his revenge. This is his way of proving that "he will not be had" (*Myth* 105). Later Camus adds: "Why kill oneself and leave this world after having won freedom" (108)? This is the existentialist consequence of the absurd that Camus and Percy knew so well: one is condemned to freedom. Will's father cannot accept the harrowing "wager" of absurd freedom and chooses suicide instead. Using Sartre's terminology, Coles notes why someone like Ed Barrett cannot accept freedom and chooses suicide:

> Man's distinctive freedom, not unqualified, but nevertheless his alone, at least on this earth, terrifies each of us. We prefer to join our very nature, the *pour-soi*, to that larger *thereness*, the fixity and certainty of the *en-soi*. Better to be a helpless or predictable "thing" in someone's scheme than to take our chances as individuals with will and the capacity to use it, with ideals and the responsibility to uphold them. (*Search* 185)

The above is an expression of Sartre's account of anguish in the face of our freedom and our desire to escape that freedom in the opacity of thingness.[19] Percy comes quite close to this existentialist theme in describing Will's contingency in the world. As an adult, after fully remembering the fateful night, Will's final realization of his father's suicide is expressed in important symbolic terms: as Will looks at and touches the tiny iron horsehead of the hitching post in front of his family home where his aunts now live, he reflects:

> *Wait.* While his finger explored the juncture of iron and bark, his eyes narrowed as if he caught a glimmer of light on the cold iron skull. *Wait.* I think he was wrong and that he was looking in the wrong place. No, not he but the times. The times were wrong and one looked in the wrong place. [...] *Wait.* He had missed it! It was not in the Brahms that one looked and not in solitariness and not in the old sad poetry but—he wrung out his ear—but here, under your nose, here in the very curiousness and drollness and extraness of the iron and the bark [...]. (260)

Contrary to Roquentin who was trying to escape into the past, Will was trying to escape from the past, into the transcendence of possibility. Once Will realizes he has been living in bad faith (his failure to recognize that he gives meaning to the past), his freedom becomes apparent to him. He now takes control of his life and moves forward by trying to help others. In accordance with Camus's notion that "the absurd depends as much on man as on the world," Linda Hobson describes the "bond" that is formed between a human and the world, as she describes Percy's symbols of iron and bark:

> The iron symbolizes the man-made world of art and industry— the world subject to time and change. The bark, however, is nature—timeless and eternal. In the union of the two Will sees the figure of a reality his father missed. In the union of high ideas with the limits imposed by nature an important bond is formed.[20]

Will understands that one's salvation doesn't come through art (music or poetry) as his father falsely believed, which is very reminiscent of Camus's statement that "art is not a refuge for the absurd," nor does it "offer an escape for the intellectual ailment" (*Myth* 95). (This also typifies Camus's rejection of the ending of *Nausea*.) Will sees his father's suicide as a mistake and takes up a vigil in the attic. This lucidity of Will's contingency is symbolized by the light in the attic: "For two hours he sat so, wakeful and alert, while his eyes followed the yellow drizzle of light into every corner of the attic room" (261). In this way, confronting the past on his own terms, Will rejects his father's outmoded, stoical views of past Southern life. Freed from his past, Will can now seek out Sutter and Jamie since Sutter has strategically left his Esso map, casebook, and hypnotic suggestion to "come and see me," so I can lend "help."

As Will approaches Santa Fe, where Sutter has taken Jamie to die with dignity and full awareness of his existence, everydayness no longer plagues Will: although "it is always Wednesday afternoon" in Mississippi, it is not so in New Mexico because "each passing second was packaged in cottony silence" (278). This signals Will's confrontation with Sutter, the denouement of the novel, and Will's self-discovery through personal interaction with other people.

Roaming around Santa Fe, Will catches sight of Sutter coming out of a drug store. Learning that Jamie is in a hospital and very near death, Will hurries to his bedside. Will is attentive to his every need as they play cards, talk, and Will brings him books and snack foods: "His illness was the sort which allows one to draw closer to oneself. Already Jamie had discovered the small privileges and warmths of invalidism" (288). Just before Jamie dies, Will remembers everything, including the hypnotic suggestion by Sutter, and tries to form a fraternal bond with the troubled doctor. Instead of seeing Sutter as a gifted doctor, Will now sees him as a failure because of his suicidal tendencies, reminding Will of his father. Also noteworthy is the fact that Ed, in his suicide, had aimed the shotgun at his heart, while Sutter has tried, unsuccessfully of course, to shoot himself in the head, relating once again to the head/heart dichotomy of Unamuno and reflecting the absurd. In other words, Ed is all heart, whereas Sutter is all head, so both are incomplete: they lack Unamuno's synthesis of head and heart. Sutter and Will's interaction at this point is important:

> If I do outlive Jamie [...], it will not be by more than two hours. What in Christ's name do you think I'm doing out here? Do you think I'm staying? Do you think I'm going back?
> The engineer opened his mouth but said nothing. For the first time in his life he was astonished. (303)

Will's astonishment is the same as Camus's "void" where one replies "nothing" when asked a sincere question. Living completely in good faith for the first time in his life, Will confronts the absurd unabashedly and does not turn away. After Will's astonishment, Sutter immediately replies: "You won't join me, Barrett," and Will replies, "No. No, thanks." Will's self-discovery becomes immanent: "Perhaps this moment more than any other, the moment of his first astonishment, marked the beginning for the engineer of what is called a normal life" (304). Will's revolt against suicide reaffirms

Camus's conclusion:

> In its way, suicide settles the absurd. It engulfs the absurd in the
> same death. But I know that in order to keep alive, the absurd
> cannot be settled. It escapes suicide to the extent that it is simul-
> taneously awareness and rejection of death. (*Myth* 54)

This also typifies Camus's notion of death: "The absurd and the extra life it
involves *therefore do not depend on man's will*, but on its contrary, which is
death" (*Myth* 63).

As Will comforts Jamie, who is progressively getting closer to death, Val
Vaught, Jamie's older sister, charges Will, over the telephone, to get the
teenager baptized before he dies. Will enlists the aid of Father Boomer, and,
acting as interpreter between the priest and teenager, helps Jamie to receive
his last rites of extreme unction. Just as Will has helped Jamie to die with
dignity, so Will does the same for Sutter in life, because Sutter is the reverse
of Ed Barrett's idealism: Sutter is all objectivity due to science. Sutter, in his
casebook, thinks that people are dispossessed, and the only way to reclaim
the world is through "lewdness." This typifies Sutter's failed marriage with
Rita and why he seeks one-night stands with other women. Sutter, like Don
Juan, tries to multiply what he cannot unify. When lewdness fails Sutter, all
he thinks he has left is suicide. Again Sutter's casebook proves prophetic:

> You [Val] are wrong too about the sinfulness of suicide in this
> age, at last the nurtured possibility of suicide, for the certain
> availability of death is the very condition of recovering oneself.
> But death is as outlawed now as sin used to be. Only one's own
> suicide remains to one. My "suicide" followed the breakdown
> of the sexual as a mode of reentry from the posture of transcen-
> dence. (291)

When Will connects with Sutter, true intersubjectivity is attained. By intersubjectivity I mean the individual self's relationships with others. If one is
to be completely human, a person must actively participate in being with
other individuals who are in the world, making oneself available to their
needs and vice versa. The "I" then evolves into a "we" rather than an objectified "him" or "her." Will's desire to be with others in the immanent world
balances his facticity and transcendence by creating a dynamic tension
against his desire for pure transcendence or wanting only to be a voyeur in
life. As Mary Howland (46) notes: "Will's [past] desire 'to know without

being known' preclude[d] attaining intersubjectivity, for it is only through participation in being and the affirmation of self that he can, through the other, discover his identity." The former void in his life becomes a revelation for Will as he enters fully into an authentic existence with others. Will's comments to Sutter expresses some possible concrete intersubjective relationships that the two men may have in common:

> It is better to do something than do nothing [...]. It is good to have a family [...]. Better to love and be loved. [...] To cultivate whatever talents one has. [...] To make a contribution, however small. [...] To do one's best to promote tolerance and understanding between the races [...]. It is better to make love to one's wife than to monkey around with a lot of women. (300)

Will's nobility as a gentleman-hero is now manifest in his revolt against suicide, the freedom to choose what his past means, and a passion for life and other people (defined by responsible, caring actions): the three consequences of the absurd.

After Jamie's death, Sutter jumps into his Edsel (a symbol of failure, linking man and machine together) and heads home to shoot himself. Will cries out "Wait," as he once cried out to his father. Will tells Sutter: "Dr. Vaught, I need you. I, Will Barrett" (318). The connection to Meursault as being the only Christ that we deserve, upholding the human condition by having the courage to live on his own terms, is manifest in the play on words: "I will bear it." Will is willing to bear, support, and help Sutter in life, if the doctor grants him the opportunity to do so. Will continues: "I need you more than Jamie needed you. Jamie had Val too." With Percy's ideas of intersubjectivity as an answer to everydayness and homelessness, the novel ends on an open note: "The Edsel paused, sighed, and stopped. Strength flowed like oil into his [Will's] muscles and he ran with great joyous ten-foot antelope bounds. The Edsel waited for him" (319).

The ambiguous, albeit positive, ending can be made clearer if I return to Percy's "The Man on the Train":

> What causes anxiety in the one is the refuge from anxiety in the other. For example, speaking objectively-empirically, it is often said that it is no wonder people are anxious nowadays, what with the possibility that the bomb might fall any minute. The Bomb would seem to be sufficient reason for anxiety; yet as it happens the reverse is the truth. The contingency "what if the

Bomb should fall?" is not only not a cause of anxiety in the alienated man but is one of his few remaining refuges from it [...]. The real anxiety question, the question no one asks because no one wants to, is the reverse: What if the Bomb should *not* fall? What then? (84)

Using Sutter and Will as examples—Sutter is the objectivist-empiricist person who asks "what if the Bomb should fall?" and Will is the person who asks "what if the Bomb should *not* fall?" (the absurd hero's position)—the ending becomes clearer: if the Bomb should *not* fall, then everything is possible within human terms, because people are hoping in spite of everything to construct authentic intersubjective relationships; therefore, there is no need for violence and destruction to ourselves or others. In a world that is rife with tension, hate, and loneliness, alternatives must be sought so that we can continue to live together in peace, friendship, and love. This makes sense if we look at Percy's epigraph for *The Last Gentleman* which is taken from Romano Guardini's *The End of the World*:

> We know now that the modern world is coming to an end...at the same time, the unbeliever will emerge from the fogs of secularism. He will cease to reap benefit from the values and forces developed by the very Revelation he denies.... Loneliness in faith will be terrible. Love will disappear from the face of the public world, but the more precious will be that love which flows from one lonely person to another...the world to come will be filled with animosity and danger, but it will be a world open and clear.

This is Percy's message to alienated people who are contemplating suicide. *Wait* is the watchword for both Percy and Camus: one must wait, not commit suicide, and see what may happen next in the world: this includes an authentic relationship with another person whether or not the Bomb should fall.

NOTES

1 John Hardy, *The Fiction of Walker Percy* (Chicago: Illinois UP, 1987) 1-2.

2 Albert Camus, *The Myth of Sisyphus and Other Essays*, trans. Justin O'Brien (New York: Alfred A. Knopf, 1972) 16.

3 On this point, see Lewis Lawson's definition of Percy's "everydayness" in *Following Percy: Essays on Walker Percy's Work* (New York: Whitson Pub. Co., 1988) 23-25.

4 See my discussion of these characteristics in CHAPTER V.

5 Walker Percy, "The Man on the Train," *The Message in the Bottle* (New York: Farrar, Straus, and Giroux, 1975) 89.

6 Walker Percy, *The Last Gentleman* (New York: Farrar, Straus, and Giroux, 1966) 68. In further references to this work in CHAPTER VI, I will use page numbers only.

7 Martin Luschei, *The Sovereign Wayfarer: Walker Percy's Diagnosis of the Malaise* (Baton Rouge: Louisiana State UP, 1972) 141.

8 See CHAPTER II and my discussion of the "look."

9 On this point see CHAPTER IV.

10 Mary Howland, *The Gift of the Other* (Pittsburgh: Duquesne UP, 1990) 61.

11 Jerome Taylor, *In Search of Self: Life, Death and Walker Percy* (Cambridge, Mass.: Cowley, 1986) 112.

12 See CHAPTER IV for my definition of this term.

13 Robert Coles, *Walker Percy: An American Search* (Boston and Toronto: Little, Brown and Co., 1978) 176.

14 Lewis Lawson and Victor Kramer, eds., *Conversations with Walker Percy* (Jackson: Mississippi UP, 1983) 12; 245-46.

15 On this point see CHAPTER IV and my discussion of Meursault and mechanical living on a typical Sunday afternoon.

16 Walker Percy, "The Message in the Bottle," *The Message in the*

NOTES

Bottle (New York: Gerard, Straus, and Giroux, 1975) 143.

[17] Jean-Paul Sartre, *Nausea*, trans. Lloyd Alexander (New York: New Directions Publishing Corp., 1964) 65.

[18] Panthea Broughton, *The Art of Walker Percy* (Baton Rouge: Louisiana State UP, 1979) 103.

[19] See my discussion of being *de trop* in CHAPTER III.

[20] Linda Hobson, *Understanding Walker Percy* (Columbia: South Carolina UP, 1988) 64.

CHAPTER VII

CONCLUSION

In *The Myth of Sisyphus* Camus states:

> The feeling of the absurd is not, for all that, the notion of the ab-
> surd. It lays the foundations for it, and that is all. It is not lim-
> ited to that notion, except in the brief moment when it passes
> judgment on the universe. Subsequently it has a chance of go-
> ing further. It is alive; in other words, it must die or else rever-
> berate. So it is with the themes we have gathered together. But
> there again what interests me is not works or minds, criticism of
> which would call for another form and another place, but the
> discovery of what their conclusions have in common.[1]

If this statement is true, some discussion of the common conclusions all of
the aforementioned existentialist writers have arrived at is necessary. To be
conscious of the absurd, for these authors, is a unique way of living and
feeling, motivating their passion for more life, which manifests itself in their
ability to create. Because each of these authors has the ability to create, fiction arises, and values can be inferred from the work of art. The consequences of an acute awareness of the absurd—revolt, freedom, and passion
for life—give rise to ethical values, which, as I have demonstrated in the
previous chapters, are concretized in each of their novels. For example, both
Augusto and Roquentin passionately wanted to be while facing an indifferent or sometimes threatening world; Meursault and Bigger revolted against

society in order to proclaim their individuality; and Will pursued his freedom to travel and choose life on his terms in order to make an authentic, intersubjective relationship with another person. Through the aforementioned protagonists' actions, values are created upon the matrix of the absurd.

In the second paragraph of Camus's essay, he states categorically that we must seek out the questions which concern life's meaning; and he goes on to say that one must approach this urgency very delicately, using both "common sense and understanding" (4). Elsewhere Camus also states that people must be in "harmony with themselves" (6); and those who do not observe the contradictory relationship between themselves and the world, are not maintaining an "equilibrium" (60).

The above statements illuminate all of the existentialist novelists whom I have discussed thus far. The absurd expresses a contradiction, which is an inescapable part of our lives. By writing about it in relation to such personal themes as the search for love, self-realization, self-creation, or friendship, fiction becomes a sympathetic self-projection into the object of contemplation: our being-in-the-world. As the gap between an individual and the world (other people included) widens, it becomes necessary to narrow this gap, providing some type of balance, so that suicide is not the result. The balance is achieved by these writers when they employ common sense and understanding in their fiction. For example, we all struggle with the same contradictions: hope and despair, duration and death, normality and abnormality, isolation and togetherness. When these authors describe these conflicts in fiction, their work forms a bond between us, the fictional characters, and the authors themselves, because we all share the same contradictions, the same climate of the absurd. Camus suggests this idea when he says: "In the fictional world in which awareness of the real world is keenest, can I remain faithful to the absurd [...]? There are thus gods of light and idols of mud. But it is essential to find the middle path leading to the faces of man" (102-03).

Since reason can take us only so far on this "middle path," we must feel the rest of our way with our passions. This is Unamuno's head/heart dichotomy, which must be harmonized, like the struggle of Augusto Perez in *Mist*. The absurd in this sense is a recognition of the blend of scorn and acceptance, rebellion and powerlessness, defiance and repetition, resolved through an affirmation of life and a balance between the opposites. The truth in living an absurd life, Camus asserts, lies somewhere between these opposites. We must accept ourselves for who we are and the world for what it is, by trying to harmonize the two. The absurd represents both a serious attitude which, on the one hand, acknowledges the faults in humans which may cause sorrow, and holds onto that, while at the same time affirming those human qualities that bring us happiness.

Absurdity depends on the fact that each one of us can find the world intelligible in some way through an understanding of the patterns of bad faith that beset us. But for this fact to become intelligible, it must be a renewed determination through shared experience. For example, those of us who have not shared the experience of a Bigger Thomas—the moral absurdity, the oppression, the chaos, and the irrationality of it—can never fully understand what it was like. But through their fictional portrayals, these authors can make us understand others, ourselves, and our world a little better, leading us toward a life in good faith. By exposing our foibles through fiction, we are led to ask ourselves questions about the search for love, self-realization, self-creation, or friendship.

Germaine Brée says that since we are given the sense of the absurd, we must learn how "profitably to live with it, transforming it into a positive incentive to live lucidly and to create."[2] This is what these authors have accomplished: through an absurd sensitivity, they offer a source of self-recognition, which gives a person an authentic existence. In other words, through the work of art in conjunction with the absurd, these authors have revealed how profoundly different the outer appearances of life are from what takes place inside the human mind. If life is a formless flux, as revealed through such characters as Augusto, Roquentin, Meursault, Bigger, and Will, the absurd offers one way to give life meaning. The absurd stops the congealment or solidification of our consciousness, induced by mechanical living, and strips reality bare so we can view life without wearing blinders. The absurd makes us acutely aware that we are in a constant state of becoming, complete with risks and choices, and, hence, freedom. Only in this way can we maintain our honesty, lucidity, and dignity. The absurd writer is in continual search for some answers, and sometimes finds these answers in common human struggle.

Camus once said that "the great novelists are philosophical novelists—that is, the contrary of thesis-writers" (101). This statement is certainly true because a novelist-philosopher's works are not always immediately understandable in thesis form, but can be grasped more readily by the philosophically untrained through fiction. The existentialist novelists I have examined are describing common themes, using the absurd, and these themes are fictional ways of reaching an audience. One must consider that Miguel de Unamuno, Jean-Paul Sartre, Albert Camus, Richard Wright, and Walker Percy put into their fiction the same themes they treat, elsewhere, in treatise form: *Mist* enhances *The Tragic Sense of Life*; *Nausea*, *Being and Nothingness*; *The Stranger*, *The Myth of Sisyphus*; *Native Son*, "How

'Bigger' Was Born"; and *The Last Gentleman, The Message in the Bottle.*
It is not by accident that these writers chose this method of inquiry, because the novel has its special characteristics. As Camus notes,

> [T]he lead taken by the novel over poetry and the essay merely represents, despite appearances, a greater intellectualization of the art. [...] The novel has its logic, its reasoning, its intuition, and its postulates. It also has its requirements of clarity. (100)

Elsewhere Camus also says of fiction: "For the absurd man it is not a matter of explaining and solving, but of experiencing and describing" (94). The novel, then, describes certain aspects of human existence that philosophy can only explain objectively, and, possibly, cannot make existentially understandable, unless one is particularly schooled in that field. The novel, therefore, provides one aspect of human experience where ideas do not replace people, and human experience is not lost. Camus explains it best in these terms: "It teaches that a man defines himself by his make-believe as well as by his sincere impulses" (11).
If the above is true, the existentialists, concerned with existence first and thought as a complement to existence, are unmistakably concerned about fiction: it promotes the principles of our commitment to responsibility, freedom, and engagement in our culture more readily than in a philosophical essay which may seem remote from life. All of the existentialist writers that I have discussed thus far have had a dual function: they did not confine themselves to objective philosophy, but also turned their talent to creative fiction in order to express their ideas. Moreover, the opportunity to write in this dual capacity is part of the broader commitment of an existentialist writer. Camus, like these other writers, could not fully express existence through philosophical essays, but elected to express it "indirectly" through fiction, hoping to recreate in his readers experiences similar to those which he has found relevant in his life. As Camus notes, "The work of art embodies a drama of the intelligence, but it proves this indirectly. [...] The true work of art is always on the human scale. It is essentially the one that says 'less'" (97-98). Creation, through fiction, becomes paramount to these authors because it furthers their task in describing their existence in the world, enhancing their acute awareness and fixity in life.
Camus says that "the last few pages of a book are already contained in the first pages" (11). With this quotation in mind, I can now address the ending of *The Myth of Sisyphus.* If my entire discussion has been to explore the absurd as described in *The Myth of Sisyphus,* then, the last pages of Camus's

essay, a narrative of the mythological Sisyphus, are relevant in uniting all of these existentialist novels.

In the beginning of Camus's narrative, he summarizes the plight of Sisyphus: Sisyphus had a certain degree of jocularity in response to the gods, for he betrayed their secrets. Because of this, the gods condemned him perpetually to roll a rock up a hill in the underworld which eventually rolled back down. The gods concluded that this futile and hopeless task was a just punishment for his defiance.

My first reference to this narrative is in *The Stranger*, regarding Meursault's trial and condemnation. In *The Myth of Sisyphus*, Camus describes the events which led up to Sisyphus's downfall in terms Meursault might have understood:

> Aegina, the daughter of Aesopus, was carried off by Jupiter. The father was shocked by that disappearance and complained to Sisyphus. He, who knew of the abduction, offered to tell about it on condition that Aesopus would give water to the citadel of Corinth. To the celestial thunderbolts he preferred the benediction of water. He was punished for this in the underworld. (119)

Could it be that the lightning bolts, a symbol of intense heat and death, are similar to the alienating qualities of the sun in *The Stranger*? If this is the case, then both Sisyphus and Meursault passionately prefer water, a symbol of life, to heat or death: Sisyphus wants water for the city of Corinth and Meursault enjoys swimming in the sea. Also both men are willing to revolt against any authority—Meursault resists bourgeois society and Sisyphus resists the Olympian gods—to assert their individuality. Their commitment to the freedom to choose life on their own terms is in contrast to the collective authoritarian pressure for conformity. Society's determination to punish them results in the guillotine for Meursault, or, in Sisyphus's case, the gods dispatched Mercury to snatch the arrogant man and, by force, lead him back to the darkness of the underworld.

The consequence of revolt, a response to the absurd, by Sisyphus and Meursault applies equally well to Unamuno's protagonist in *Mist*: Augusto Perez; yet the consequence of passion (another response to the absurd), in relation to creation, is the best theme for comparing *Mist* to Camus's narrative at the end of *The Myth of Sisyphus*. After Camus explains that Sisyphus is the "absurd hero" because of his "scorn of the gods, his hatred of death, and his passion for life" (120), Camus goes on to say, "this is the price that must be paid for the passions of this earth. Nothing is told us about Sisyphus in the underworld. Myths are made for the imagination to breathe life into them" (120). Unamuno says something strikingly similar in *Mist*. Augusto has gone to see Unamuno in Salamanca to tell the author that he will commit suicide. Unamuno protests and says this idea of Augusto's is preposterous since he is only a character in a "nivola." In relation to the above passage from Camus's narrative, Unamuno and Augusto's remarks are worth noting:

> "No, you don't exist any more than any other creature of fic-
> tion exists. You are not, my poor Augusto, anything more than
> a figment of my imagination and of my readers' imagination
> [...]."
> "Look here, Don Miguel...are you sure you're not mistaken
> and everything that's happening to me is the exact reverse of
> what you think and have told me?"[3]

The paradoxical nature of these two statements by Unamuno and Augusto show us Unamuno's commitment to creativity: it is a necessary function in life and gives him a sense of authentic being. Unamuno once wrote that "every man, really a man, is the son of a legend, written or oral. And there is nothing but legend or, in other words, novel."[4] In essence, Camus and Unamuno are basically saying the same thing about art and the imagination. Camus sums it up best when he says that "the absurd joy par excellence is creation." Since joy is a passion—one of the consequences of the absurd—then, one way to express this joy, which is also a positive response to the absurd, is by creating a work of art. Camus statement that "myths are made for the imagination," may explain Augusto and Unamuno's dispute over the truth of their personal existence. It also suggests the head/heart dichotomy of the absurd, so reminiscent of Unamuno's tragic sense of life and his quest for immortality. In *Amor y pedagogía*, one of Unamuno's characters says: "From what source was art born? From the thirst for immortality."[5]

The characters of Augusto and Sisyphus are alive in our imagination; and since our imagination is part of our being, there is a subtle connection between a character and an author. Fictional creation and self-creation are inextricably bound together: a person who seeks an authentic, passionate existence, using the imagination to create a work of art, finds his or her own existence enhanced. In other words, while Don Quijote has his own reality as myth or fiction—this peculiar knight-errant transcends the ages because of his unique character—so does Cervantes since he created Don Quijote. In this way, art can replenish and revitalize the human spirit; art helps to keep the tension between oneself and the world, between oneself and others, and between an author and character.

Camus describes Sisyphus, straining to push his rock uphill; as rock and man reach the top, the stone rushes back down to where Sisyphus will have to return and push it uphill again:

> It is during that return, that pause, that Sisyphus interests me. A face that toils so close to stones is already stone itself! I see that man going back down with a heavy yet measured step toward the torment of which he will never know the end. That hour like a breathing-space which returns as surely as his suffering, that is the hour of consciousness. At each of those moments when he leaves the heights and gradually sinks toward the lairs of the gods, he is superior to his fate. He is stronger than his rock. (121)

The epiphany that Roquentin, in *Nausea*, has in the park, concerning the "in-itself" (objects in the world) and the "for-itself" (human consciousness), has much in common with this passage by Camus. The play on words in Camus's narrative, "A face that toils so closely to stones is already stone *itself*" [my emphasis], suggests Sartre's dynamic tension between the in-itself (the rock) and the for-itself (Sisyphus). Roquentin's realization that his being-in-the-world is absurd, that he is contingent or "in the way" unless he takes control of his life and moves forward, is summed up for us as Sartre describes Roquentin looking at the roots of a chestnut tree and existence unveiling itself. The roots of the tree (the in-itself) are comparable to Sisyphus's rock; and Roquentin's "horrible ecstasy" of his contingency (he is feeling *de trop*) as he stares at these roots smacks of Sisyphus, full of "torment" and "suffering," returning to his rock. This is the "hour of consciousness," or Sisyphus's realization that he is *de trop*. In other words, the rock is indifferent to Sisyphus's demands that it stay at the top of this hill, and Sisyphus's recognition of this fact reveals the absurd rift between himself and nature; however, he does have the ability to interpret his relationship to the indifferent rock, create his own meaning in life, and this is why he is "superior" or "stronger than his rock." This conveys to us Sisyphus's freedom to choose.

Both Camus and Sartre, describing Sisyphus and Roquentin in these particular situations, are making freedom, as one confronts the absurd in these particular contexts, primary to the existentialist writer's task. Consequently, Camus's depiction of Sisyphus being "condemned" to "ceaselessly rolling a rock to the top of a mountain," can be compared to Sartre's assertion that we are condemned to freedom and must perpetually confront our inescapable choices.

Camus continues his narrative by saying:

> If this myth is tragic, that is because its hero is conscious. [...] Sisyphus, proletarian of the gods, powerless and rebellious, knows the whole extent of his wretched condition: it is what he thinks of during his descent. The lucidity that was to constitute his torture at the same time crowns his victory. There is no fate that cannot be surmounted by scorn. (121)

This description of Sisyphus's plight also parallels that of Richard Wright's Bigger Thomas. When Camus speaks of Sisyphus as a member of the proletariat, one is reminded of Bigger's position as a Negro in America. Like the gods who have banished Sisyphus to the role of a common laborer, Bigger is limited by white society to menial jobs—a chauffeur for the rich Dalton family—so his family can eat. Mr. Dalton gives Bigger a job, hoping to give Negroes a chance, and donates millions of dollars to black organizations; but he squeezes money from Bigger's family by renting them a rat-infested apartment, on Chicago's South Side, at an exorbitant rate. Also Mr. Dalton won't lower his rates for Negroes or allow them to live in any other section of the city (like the gods who have restricted Sisyphus's freedom of movement to a particular hill), because he considers it unethical to underbid his competitors or desegregate the racial classes, restricting their freedom of movement. In this way, Mr. Dalton, and by implication any oppressive or dominant society, hopes to keep the social hierarchy at status quo. Bigger, like Sisyphus, is powerless to stop this system, but is nevertheless rebellious and contemptuous of it. Bigger's revolt is the acknowledgment of a dreadful fate, without the resignation that should accompany it. Bigger's scorn of white society is his consciousness of the absurd, and his realization that he lives in a "No Man's Land." This scorn is an all-consuming passion which leads to his revolt and his acts of murder. Passion and revolt, free choices once again, are two consequences of the absurd which become central to Wright's novel, as they were in Camus's narrative.

Finally, let us examine *The Last Gentleman* and the affinities it has with Camus's narrative. Camus states:

> When the images of earth cling too tightly to memory, when the call of happiness becomes too insistent, it happens that melan-

choly rises in man's heart: this is the rock's victory [...]. The
boundless grief is too heavy to bear. [...] But crushing truths
perish from being acknowledged. Thus, Oedipus at the outset
obeys fate without knowing it. But from the moment he knows,
his tragedy begins. Yet at the same moment, blind and desper-
ate, he realizes that the only bond linking him to the world is
the cool hand of a girl. Then a tremendous remark rings out:
[...] all is well." (122)

First, with Camus's use of such phrases as "melancholy rises in man's heart"
and "the boundless grief is too heavy to bear," this is similar to Percy's description of Will Barrett's "alienation"; and Camus's "images of earth,"
which "cling too tightly" in our memories and become the "rock's victory,"
remind one of Will's "homelessness": the incommensurability between Will
and nature which makes him feel out of place in this world. It is also plausi-
ble to say that Will Barrett's "crushing truths," which "perish from being acknowledged," concern the memory of his father's suicide. That return to the
past—Will standing in front of his old family home in Ithaca and looking at
the iron horsehead of the hitching post—allows him to overcome his amnesia, similar to Oedipus obeying his fate "without knowing it." The resolution
Will finds in accepting his past—and the absurdity of his life—suggests a
similar affirmation. Two paragraphs later, Camus says something which relates so well to Will returning home, confronting his past, and coming to
terms with death:

At the subtle moment when man glances backward over his life,
Sisyphus returning toward his rock, in that slight pivoting he
contemplates that series of unrelated actions which become his
fate, created by him, combined under his memory's eye and
soon sealed by his fate. (123)

After confronting his father's suicide, Will now moves forward with his
life and tries to make authentic intersubjective relationships with other people, responding to their needs. Like Oedipus who is linked to the world by
the touch of a girl, Will helps Jamie Vaught die with dignity and attempts to
befriend the suicidal Sutter Vaught after Jamie dies. The watchword "Wait"
that Will yells out to Sutter suggests Oedipus's realization that "all is well."
Will is attempting to overcome the loneliness in his life through a bond with
another person. It is Will's passion for life, another response to the absurd,
and his desire to be with other people that sums up this novel in terms simi-

lar to Camus's narrative.

Now I can specifically address the issue of whether or not any positive results can come from these descriptions and experiences of the absurd. Camus says of Sisyphus's toil:

> If the descent is thus sometimes performed in sorrow, it can also take place in joy. This word is not too much. Again I fancy Sisyphus returning toward his rock, and the sorrow was in the beginning. [...] Happiness and the absurd are two sons of the same earth. They are inseparable.(121-22)

All is not despair and anguish as one confronts the absurd because happiness and joy can be a product of it. In retrospect, the balance and harmony that Camus describes in the first half of *The Myth of Sisyphus* is now fully apparent: a person can experience sorrow from the absurd, but can also experience happiness.

Is joy or sorrow dominant in these aforementioned novels? A close analysis of each of these novels endings will also provide a clue. Augusto, "with a smile in his eyes," mocks Unamuno and tells the author that he too will die; Meursault opens his "heart" to "the benign indifference of the universe" and realizes that he is "happy"; Roquentin, feels "joy" as he listens to music, and he decides to write a novel so he can remember his "life without repugnance"; Bigger clutches the bars in his cell, and he waits for his execution with a "faint, wry, bitter smile"; and Will tries to prevent Sutter from killing himself and "laugh[s]" with relief because he can possibly "live like other men—rejoin the human race." These examples indicate that distinct human emotions point to a positive side of the absurd. Camus's final paragraph in his narrative sums up this point and demonstrates what all of these existentialist authors have been striving for in their descriptions, notions and experiences of the absurd:

> I leave Sisyphus at the foot of the mountain! One always finds one's burden again. But Sisyphus teaches the higher fidelity that negates gods and raises rocks. He too concludes that all is well. [...] The struggle itself toward the heights is enough to fill a man's heart. One must imagine Sisyphus happy. (123)

Through the method of fiction—"the struggle"—which is the sympathetic self-projection in the face of the absurd, all is now complete. Because of the conflict between our desire for meaning and the silence of the world, fictional creation is born; and this becomes an honest confrontation with the absurd. Creation gives one strength and courage to meet the absurd by a positive reaching out to each person through literature and art. We must, therefore, imagine all of these protagonists happy, having won their freedom through revolt and a passion for living.

NOTES

[1] Albert Camus, *The Myth of Sisyphus and Other Essays*, trans. Justin O'Brien (New York: Alfred A. Knopf, 1975) 28. In further references to this work in CHAPTER VII, I will use page numbers only.

[2] Germaine Brée, *Albert Camus* (New York: Columbia UP, 1964) 28.

[3] Miguel de Unamuno, *Mist, Novela/Nivola*, trans. Anthony Kerrigan (Princeton: Princeton UP, 1976) 219.

[4] Miguel de Unamuno, *Obras completas*. 2nd ed., 16 vols. (Madrid: Afrodisio Aguado, 1958) 10: 916. [translation mine]

[5] Miguel de Unamuno, *Amor y pedagogía, Obras completas*. 2nd ed., 16 vols. (Madrid: Afrodisio Aguado, 1958) 2: 546. [translation mine]

BIBLIOGRAPHY

Barnes, Hazel. *An Existentialist Ethics*. New York: Alfred A. Knopf, 1967.

———. *Humanistic Existentialism*. Lincoln: Nebraska UP, 1956.

———. *Sartre*. New York: J. B. Lippincott Co., 1973.

Binkley, Luther. *Conflict of Ideals: Changing Values in Western Society*. New York: Van Nostrand/Reynolds Co., 1969.

Blocker, H. Gene. *Metaphysics of Absurdity*. Washington D.C.: America UP, 1979.

Bone, Robert. *Richard Wright*. Minneapolis: Minnesota UP, 1969.

———· "Richard Wright." *Twentieth Century Interpretations of Native Son*. Ed. Houston Baker. Englewood Cliffs, N. J.: Prentice-Hall Inc., 1972.

Brée, Germaine. *Albert Camus*. New York: Columbia UP, 1964.

———. *Camus: A Collection of Critical Essays*. Englewoods Cliffs, N. J.: Prentice-Hall Inc., 1962.

Broughton, Panthea. *The Art of Walker Percy*. Baton Rouge: Louisiana State UP, 1979.

Camus, Albert. *Lyrical and Critical Essays*. Trans. Ellen Kennedy. Ed.

Philip Thody. New York: Alfred A. Knopf, 1968.

———. "Non, je ne suis pas existentialist." *Les Nouvelles Littéraires* 15 Nov. 1945: 1+.

———· *The Myth of Sisyphus and Other Essays.* Trans. Justin O'Brien. New York: Alfred A. Knopf, 1972.

———· *The Stranger.* Trans. Stuart Gilbert. New York: Vintage Books, 1954.

Catalano, Joseph. *A Commentary of Jean-Paul Sartre's Being and Nothingness.* Chicago: Chicago and London UP, 1974.

Coles, Robert. *Walker Percy: An American Search.* Boston and Toronto: Little, Brown and Co., 1978.

Cruickshank, John. *Albert Camus and the Literature of Revolt.* London: Oxford UP, 1960.

Doubrovsky, Serge. "The Ethics of Albert Camus." *Critical Essays on Albert Camus.* Ed. Robert Lecker. Boston: G. K. Hall & Co., 1988.

Eastman, Max. *Sense of Humor.* New York: Charles Scribner's Sons, 1921.

Ellis, Robert. *The Tragic Pursuit of Being: Unamuno and Sartre.* Tuscaloosa and London: Alabama UP, 1988.

Ellison, David. *Understanding Albert Camus.* Columbia, South Carolina: South Carolina UP, 1990.

Fishburn, Katherine. *Richard Wright's Hero: The Faces of a Rebel-Victim.* Metuchen, N. J.: The Scarecrow Press, Inc., 1977.

Fisher, Dorothy. "Introduction to the First Edition." *Twentieth Century Interpretations of Native Son.* Ed. Houston Baker. Englewood Cliffs, N. J.: Prentice-Hall Inc., 1972.

Gibson, Donald. "Wright's Invisible Native Son." *Twentieth Century Interpretations of Native Son.* Ed. Houston Baker. Englewood Cliffs, N. J.: Prentice-Hall Inc., 1972.

Gilbert, Stuart, trans. *The Outsider.* By Albert Camus. Rpt. in *The Collected*

Fiction of Albert Camus. London: Hamish Hamilton, 1960.

Hardy, John. *The Fiction of Walker Percy*. Chicago: Illinois UP, 1987.

Hobson, Linda. *Understanding Walker Percy*. Columbia: South Carolina UP, 1988.

Howe, Irving. "Black Boys and Native Sons." *Twentieth Century Interpretations of Native Son*. Ed. Houston Baker. Englewood Cliffs, N. J.: Prentice-Hall Inc., 1972.

Howland, Mary. *The Gift of the Other*. Pittsburgh: Duquesne UP, 1990.

Jackson, Esther. "The American Negro and the Image of the Absurd." *Richard Wright: A Collection of Critical Essays*. Ed. Richard Macksey and Frank Moorer. Englewood Cliffs, N. J.: Prentice-Hall Inc., 1984.

Joyce, Joyce Ann. "The Tragic Hero." *Modern Critical Interpretations: Richard Wright's Native Son*. Ed. Harold Bloom. New York: Chelsea House Publishers, 1988.

Kierkegaard, Sören. "That Individual." *Existentialism from Dostoevsky to Sartre*. Ed. Walter Kaufmann. New York: New American Library, 1975.

———. "Truth Is Subjectivity." *Existentialism from Dostoevsky to Sartre*. Ed. Walter Kaufmann. New York: New American Library, 1975.

Lawson, Lewis, and Victor Kramer, eds. *Conversations with Walker Percy*. Jackson: Mississippi UP, 1983.

Lawson, Lewis. *Following Percy: Essays on Walker Percy's Work*. New York: Whitson Pub. Co., 1988.

Lazere, Donald. *The Unique Creation of Albert Camus*. New Haven and London: Yale UP, 1973.

Livingstone, Leon. "The Novel as Self-Creation." *Unamuno: Creator and Creation*. Ed. J. R. Barcia and M. A. Zeitlin. Los Angeles and Berkeley: U of Calif. P, 1967.

Lorenz, Konrad. *On Aggression*. New York: Harcourt, Brace, and World,

1963.

Luschei, Martin. *The Sovereign Wayfarer: Walker Percy's Diagnosis of the Malaise*. Baton Rouge: Louisiana State UP, 1972.

Macksey, Richard and Frank Moorer. "Introduction." *Richard Wright: A Collection of Critical Essays*. Englewood Cliffs, N. J.: Prentice-Hall Inc., 1984.

Madariaga, Salvador de. Introduction. *The Tragic Sense of Life*. By Miguel de Unamuno. Princeton: Princeton UP, 1972.

Margolies, Edward. *Native Sons: A Critical Study of Twentieth-Century Negro American Authors*. Philadelphia and New York: J. B. Lippincott Co., 1968.

Marias, Julian. *Miguel de Unamuno*. Trans. Frances Lopez-Morillas. Cambridge, Mass.: Harvard UP, 1966.

McCall, Dan. "The Bad Nigger." *Twentieth Century Interpretations of Native Son*. Ed. Houston Baker. Englewood Cliffs, N. J.: Prentice-Hall Inc. 1972.

McCarthy, Patrick. *Albert Camus: The Stranger*. Cambridge: Cambridge UP, 1988.

Parker, Alexander. "On the Interpretation of *Niebla*." *Unamuno: Creator and Creation*. Ed. J. R. Barcia and M. A. Zeitlin. Los Angeles and Berkeley: U of Calif. P, 1967.

Percy, Walker. *The Last Gentleman*. New York: Farrar, Straus, and Giroux, 1966.

——· "The Man on the Train." *The Message in the Bottle*. New York: Farrar, Straus, and Giroux, 1975.

——· "The Message in the Bottle." *The Message in the Bottle*. New York: Farrar, Straus, and Giroux, 1975.

Rudd, Margaret. *The Lone Heretic*. New York: Gordian P, 1976.

Sanborn, Patricia. *Existentialism*. New York: Pegasus, 1968.

Sartre, Jean-Paul. "An Explication of *The Stranger.*" *Camus: A Collection of Critical Essays.* Ed. Germaine Brée. Englewood Cliffs, N. J.: Prentice-Hall Inc., 1962.

——· *Being and Nothingness.* Trans. Hazel Barnes. New York: Philosophical Library, 1956.

——· *Essays in Existentialism.* Ed. Wade Baskin. Secaucus, N. J.: Citadel Press, 1965.

——· "Portrait of an Antisemite." *Existentialism from Dostoevsky to Sartre.* Ed. Walter Kaufmann. New York: New American Library, 1975.

——· *Nausea.* Trans. Lloyd. Alexander. New York: New Directions Publishing Corp., 1964.

——· *No Exit and Three Other Plays.* Trans. Stuart Gilbert. New York: Vintage Books, 1955.

——· *The Family Idiot.* Trans. Carol Cosman. 4 vols. Chicago and London: U of Chicago P, 1981-1991.

——· "Tribute to Albert Camus." *Critical Essays on Albert Camus.* Ed. Robert Lecker. Boston: G. K. Hall & Co., 1988.

——· *What is Literature?.* Trans. Bernard Frechtman. New York: Philosophical Library, 1949.

Shaw, Donald. *The Generation of 1898.* New York: Barnes and Noble, 1975.

Siegel, Paul. "The Conclusion of Richard Wright's *Native Son.*" *Twentieth Century Interpretations of Native Son.* Ed. Houston Baker. Englewood Cliffs, N. J.: Prentice-Hall Inc., 1972.

Skerrett, Joseph. *Modern Critical Interpretations: Richard Wright's Native Son.* New York: Chelsea House Publishers, 1988.

Stern, Alfred. "Unamuno: Pioneer of Existentialism." *Unamuno: Creator and Creation.* Ed. J. R. Barcia and M. A. Zeitlin. Los Angeles and Berkeley: U of Calif. P, 1967.

Sypher, Wylie. *Comedy: The Meanings of Comedy*. New York: Doubleday Anchor Books, 1956.

Taylor, Jerome. *In Search of Self: Life, Death and Walker Percy*. Cambridge, Mass.: Cowley, 1986.

Thody, Philip. *Albert Camus: A Biographical Study*. London: Hamish Hamilton, 1961.

——· *Jean-Paul Sartre: A Literary and Political Study*. London: Hamish Hamilton, 1972.

——· *Sartre: A Biographical Introduction*. New York: Charles Scribner's Sons, 1971.

Tisson-Braun, Micheline. "Silence and the Desert: The Flickering Vision." *Critical Essays on Albert Camus*. Ed. Robert Lecker. Boston: G. K. Hall & Co., 1988.

Unamuno, Miguel de. *Amor y pedagogía*. 2nd ed. Madrid: Afrodisio Aguado, 1958. Vol. 2 of *Obras completas*. 16 vols.

——· *How to Make a Novel. Novela/Nivola*. Trans. Anthony Kerrigan. Princeton: Princeton UP, 1976.

——· *Mist. Novela/Nivola*. Trans Anthony Kerrigan. Princeton: Princeton UP, 1976.

——· *Obras Completas*. 2nd ed. Vol. 10. Madrid: Afrodisio Aguado, 1958. 16 vols.

——. *The Tragic Sense of Life*. Trans. Anthony Kerrigan. Princeton: Princeton UP, 1972.

Webb, Constance. *Richard Wright: A Biography*. New York: G. P. Putnam's Sons, 1968.

Weber, Frances. "Unamuno's *Niebla*: From Novel to Dream." *PMLA* 87 (1973): 209.

Wilson, Colin. *The Outsider*. Boston: Houghton Mifflin Co., 1956.

Wright, Richard. "How 'Bigger' Was Born." *Native Son*. New York and

Evanston: Harper & Row, 1940.

———. *Native Son*. New York and Evanston: Harper & Row, 1940.